Pregnancy Centers;

WHY I SERVE

A
Birth Mom's
Story

GEORGIA BARNES

PREGNANCY CENTERS; WHY I SERVE
A BIRTH MOM'S STORY

iUniverse books may be ordered through booksellers or by contacting:

iUniverse
1663 Liberty Drive
Bloomington, IN 47403
www.iuniverse.com
1-800-Authors (1-800-288-4677)

ISBN: 978-1-5320-4301-7 (sc)
ISBN: 978-1-5320-4300-0 (e)

Library of Congress Control Number: 2018904440

Print information available on the last page.

iUniverse rev. date: 05/07/2018

CONTENTS

FOREWORD

I was introduced to Georgia Barnes in Indianapolis IN through our husband's mutual passion for fast cars. I knew immediately that there was something special about her. In the two days we spent together, I learned that we both have a heart for hurting people. We both have a love for the work being done at pregnancy centers and we both share a past that involved an unplanned pregnancy. We shared our hearts about some of our past but mostly talked about how God is working in our lives currently.

I was thrilled to hear about this book, the one your holding right now, and the truth that is being shared about the different aspects of the non-profit organization. Georgia being a client advocate and mentor in Indiana, and I am the executive director of a center in South Texas, our love for pregnancy centers is mutual. When I began reading this book I was immediately inspired by Georgia's involvement and understanding of this sort of outreach and captivated by her story as it unfolded throughout the pages of her journey to find healing, purpose, restoration and ultimately beautiful reunion.

I thank God for Georgia Barnes, for her courage to share her story. I know it was not easy for her to lay her heart out on these pages. I applaud the many brave women like Georgia who have stepped out on faith to share the truth, in love about their past and the journey to healing and restoration found only by trusting God. If you find yourself in the pages of this book and are feeling unsure of what to do, please know that you are not alone. I recommend that you reach out to Georgia, a trusted friend or a pregnancy center near you. But first and most importantly reach out to Jesus, He loves you.

Jeri Lynn Scott
Executive Director of Resources for Women PRC
Author of Uniquely Gifted, Called According to His Purpose

PREFACE

My heart had long been inspired to share my journey of coming to understand my own value. However, each time I tried to write the story, I became overwhelmed with too many details. It wasn't until I had moved and left my position at a pregnancy center that this project came to be.

Surprised by the misconceptions I encountered about the purpose of pregnancy centers, I decided to organize part 1 of *my* book to correspond with the questions and comments I have received from different individuals. Around this framework, I've woven my personal story as a young mother-to-be, as well as an explanation of the ministry that I have grown to love. In part 2, I've shared my current journey as a birth mom—during and after a reunion many years in the making.

My utmost desire would be that my efforts would be used as a tool to bring understanding about these types of nonprofit organizations. Perhaps reading my story will inspire you, the reader, to get involved. Or perhaps *Pregnancy Centers* will even give someone the courage to step through the doors of a center near him or her.

None of this would have been possible without my husband Bob's support. He has never questioned the time or money I spent on this endeavor. And often he has lifted me in his prayers so that I would be able to finish what my heart inspired me to do. I am forever grateful for my family and friends. Their encouragement has spurred me on to complete this project that has been hidden inside me for a long time.

My prayer is that this book will accomplish what God wants—nothing more, nothing less. It is all for His glory (Hebrews 13:20–21).

INTRODUCTION

"What is a 'pregnancy center' about, anyhow?"

"As you can plainly see, I am not ever going to need their services."

"Isn't that just for young girls who find themselves in trouble?"

"Isn't that just a pro-life thing? I don't get involved in political issues."

"I don't have any desire to partner with the local center! My daughter and her husband work hard, and they don't get anything from *those* centers."

"Why should I help? Don't pregnancy centers get enough government funds?"

Some people are afraid to ask about pregnancy centers and even believe that they are taking some sort of political stand if they get involved. One might not have vocalized questions about the ministry but have had thoughts about what these centers do. A few people might even have had a small notion to donate a dollar or two toward their local center, but the thought quickly leaves their minds, as they have other pressing things on their to-do lists.

I am a birth mom, and I will be sharing my personal thoughts on why I serve and support these types of ministries. As you read the following pages, my prayer is that a seed of compassion will be planted, which will ultimately grow into a passion to get involved in some small way.

In my own words, I'll explain what I have learned about a pregnancy center located in Michigan, as well as my own personal struggle I had at a very young age.

Please understand my heart; this is my story. It might sound similar to other stories you've heard in a lot of ways, yet it will be different. Women may have been through situations that are parallel to mine. However, we all process things differently. What a situation means to us depends on how we process our emotions, the internal dialogue that goes on inside our heads, and how we see ourselves. In no way am I saying that every birth mom's story is a carbon copy of mine. I can account only for my own personal journey of healing and pray that others will find liberation as they begin their own journeys.

Please note that in part 1 of *Pregnancy Centers* the sections pertaining to my personal story of when I was young girl will be set in a different font.

PART 1

The Love, Lessons, and Resources Parents Need: Then and Now

CHAPTER 1

Walking through the Doors

In spring 2014, I stepped up to the building that sat on the corner of Broad and Maple. It was my first time at a pregnancy center, and as I pulled the door open, I felt as if I had finally found my destiny. I believed that I had something to give, especially given the healing I had received seven years earlier.

I walked up to the friendly woman behind the counter and announced myself. "Hello," I said. "I have an appointment with the director." We had talked on the phone, and I was eager to meet the voice that I had grown to love. The excitement I felt must have been apparent because my wide smile was matched by the receptionist as she phoned the director to come meet me. Suddenly I was greeted by the tallest woman I believe I had ever met, and her beauty matched her height. She shook my hand and led me to her office, where I began to share with her my heart and how I wanted to become a volunteer.

After our conversation, she briefly explained the ministry as she gave me a tour of the facility. As I walked along, looking at the private rooms, I imagined myself sitting with different clients and sharing this unconditional love that I had found.

I was given an application and filled it out as soon as I got home. A few weeks later, I received a call from the center letting me know that I had been put on the schedule for training. I assumed training consisted of one four-hour evening. However, I quickly learned it was more involved.

Training day one

The other volunteers in my group ranged from a young college student to other women who were closer to my age. Sitting together, we explained briefly why we were choosing to get involved. As each person shared, I realized we had something in common. We wanted to give back what had been given to us—time. People had invested time in each of our situations, and we wanted to give that time to someone else in need.

I never thought much of how abortions became legalized in America. To my surprise, the history of abortion in the United States was not at all what I had thought. We also were told the statistics describing the types of clients who walked through the doors at the pregnancy center. As these things were shared, my naive enthusiasm was met with the reality of how much these individuals needed to experience nonjudgmental, unconditional love.

Although we trainees would continue to meet as a group, we were told there would be independent reading assignments. Up to that point, I'd had training in Stephen Ministries, so I really didn't think I would have new things to learn and felt sure the training would be more of a review for me.

Though, it was a few days later that I found myself feeling a little uncomfortable with my reading assignment.

I remember that day as clearly as the sky that sunny afternoon. I decided to go out on the deck to begin reading through my training manual. It resembled what I had read before, and I felt confident that I could probably push through and read the entire thing. However, I paused when I came to the place where the reader was asked, "What is the client feeling?" I felt myself travel back in time. Pondering the different scenarios painted for the trainee, I found it increasingly difficult to imagine "her" as an imaginary person.

The reading gave the following suggestions:

> *Fear* – The client may be frightened about telling her parents or partner the information that she has just learned. And looking at the future with this life-changing situation may be too overwhelming for the client.

> *Worthlessness* – The client may have suffered from a poor self-image before becoming pregnant, and the pregnancy can intensify these feelings. Her deep longing to achieve significance and worth may have led her to a pregnancy scare or an actual unplanned pregnancy, both of which would further affect her poor self-image.

As I read these descriptive feelings, something surfaced inside of me. It was as if the wind had shifted and the pages of my past had blown open. I then realized that I wasn't identifying with a fictional person. I was identifying with myself! Before I knew it, my mind took me back to when I was fifteen years old—scared, and alone. I knew full well this sense of worthlessness.

My sudden burst of emotion took me by surprise. While calming myself down, I asked Papa God: *"Are there more areas of my past that I need to explore? I thought I received healing. Are there more fragments left that need mending?"*

I truly thought I had processed all of my past and received

complete healing. But it was evident by my reaction that I might not be as "healed" as I thought. To be quite honest, this—that I had more of my past to process—was hard for me to admit to myself. But I've come to realize that in order for me to move forward I would have to allow the younger, forgotten me to have her voice.

The girl I had forgotten

Without going into the whole story about how my perception of being female became distorted, let me mention that I was the only girl of six children.

I had little girl things to play with, like my "Beautiful Crissy" doll. But I became quickly bored playing alone, combing out her red hair. After dressing my paper dolls with one-dimensional styles, I decided to leave my girlie world to join in the adventures that my brothers seemed to be having.

Ahh, my fondest memories were when I ran around like a little boy from 'never-never land,' no T-shirt, hair in a wild mess, joining my brothers (and their friends) as they hunted for insects, frogs, and snakes.

At the end of every school year, my thoughts would drift to the daylong escapades we would embark on. I loved hanging out with the gang those summer months—it was my favorite time of the year.

The boys and I would jump out of our beds early, dress, and run outside barefoot into the dew-wet grass. Excited, we could hear frogs in the far-off distance; they sounded like huge creatures lurking in the woods nearby. I would set out determined to prove my worthiness by capturing the biggest frog or longest snake. The oohs and ahs that came from the boys' mouths after I'd revealed the creatures I'd apprehended was gratifying. I felt valued and accepted. That was my driving force when I would jump into the thickest woods on my own. And once we moved out to the farm, I had an endless supply of these prize specimens.

Then one summer, I felt I had been thrown into quick sand. My heart sank when I learned that I had new rules to follow— one being I had to wear a T-shirt. I wasn't allowed to follow the guys around anymore. And when our friends came around, it became a boys-only club. I didn't understand why, and I felt rejected. How could I compete if I had no clue what captivated their attention? I didn't know how to gain their favor anymore. Tree frogs were no longer cool to look at. I didn't understand how I had gone from being one of the guys, laughing into the late hours of the night, to having the door slammed in my face.

It was a lonely time for me. I would go for walks down the long, gravel road we lived on, picking flowers and imagining myself as a lost princess. I let my heart believe that I was so important that the whole royal kingdom was out searching for me in order to bring me home.

My mom worked outside the home and was gone many hours. My dad plugged away on finishing the house, while his debilitating health continued to steal his strength. Needless to say, I was often left alone with my own thoughts.

At about the age of fourteen, I started to feel embarrassed and uneasy with how my dad diligently tried to find me a boyfriend. One night, Dad even allowed a young person to come into my bedroom to wake me up. This boy wanted to put a macramé necklace that held a blue glass eye around my neck. He'd made the necklace for me, and when he gave it to me, he tried to steal a kiss. I felt so threatened in that moment that I smacked him.

I tried to tell my dad that I was not interested in the boys that came around, but that only seemed to upset him. He told me I was a "cold fish" and that I would become a lonely, old woman if I didn't change my attitude toward the opposite sex.

To assure my dad that I did have interest in boys, I told him that I was lovesick over a person who had once been very much part of our lives. I was five years old when we first met. He came to my rescue (so to speak) when I was left alone to walk home from school, he was ten. Before we had moved away, he was a part of every frog hunting, snake catching excursion we had in those early years.

To get the silly notion out of my head that I would one day marry this boy, my father called him up and invited him to come for a visit. I figure that my dad assumed he wouldn't be interested in me, a soon-to-be fifteen-year-old girl, and that would be the end of it.

I'm not going to begin to try to understand my father's motives behind his desire for me to have a boyfriend, much less the programming he insisted I needed to learn once I did have a boyfriend. But this long-lost "knight" had me believe that I was something special.

My "prince charming" would drive several hours to be with me at least once a week throughout the summer. He told me that there was no one else like me and that I was beautiful. I had never been told that before, and I believed him.

He would often play "Time in a Bottle," and I was convinced that I was his "dream come true" and that we would be together forever.

I loved going to the mailbox at the end of our long, dirt drive during that summer and even into the early fall months. I would receive a letter every three to four days. He wrote me poems and lyrics of songs and told me how he missed being around me.

Then one day after school, I eagerly opened the last piece of mail I would ever receive from him. In that letter, he told me that he had to grow up and that I was just a kid. We'd had fun over the summer, but that was all it was—just having "fun"—and he was engaged to be married.

I couldn't believe that my knight was just going to throw me away like that. I had done everything my father had instructed me to do. I'd given this young man all of me. Yet, in the end, it wasn't good enough. And I felt even more rejected than I had before.

That same evening while at a basketball game, devastated by the shock of my "love" jilting my affections, I slipped out of the gymnasium. Feeling like an outcast, insignificant, and even used, I found myself a quiet corner where I could release the tears that I'd held back most of the day. I thought I was alone but soon realized I was being watched.

That was when I was approached by an individual I had met a few years back at a church youth group I was invited to. To tell you the truth I was surprised this person even remembered me (he was quite a bit older than me as well) but he took an interest and asked me why I was crying. We started walking as I shared the things that were heavy on my heart. I believed that this person cared about the reason I was upset. But it wasn't long before I realized his intentions. Looking up, I noticed that we had walked away from the bright high school lights to a more secluded area. His gentle gestures of concern turned into something entirely different.

The sinking feeling I felt was overwhelming. I was in shock. It was as if I had just been smacked in the face and punched in the gut all at the same time.

I felt embarrassed about all the things I'd told him. He didn't care that I was hurting and sad.

As this person made it perfectly clear what his intentions were, all my disappointments played over and over in my head.

The fairy-tale love story I had envisioned was lost like the leaves that had once grown from the now barren trees. The reality that all the wonderful words written and spoken to me by my knight—and now by this old acquaintance of mine—were meaningless hit me. And I concluded that I was nothing but a toy in the eyes of the male race.

That was when the programing I'd received and the lies I believed about myself got tangled up inside my head. I decide that my life meant nothing. I concluded that servicing the opposite sex was the only reason I had been born. That was when I gave up. I stopped trying to hold the broken pieces of my heart together. The pieces just got ground into a fine dust to be blown away in the wind, and my heart would never be the same again. I don't know when I had learned how to turn myself off, but it had become easy for me to do. That was what I did; I turned off all emotions and went numb.

I don't know why this had to happen to me. I guess I was at the wrong place at the wrong time. Or maybe this acquaintance figured I was just that kind of girl. I was scared. I didn't want to do what he wanted to do, and he knew it. He even jokingly said, "It isn't like I have a knife and I'm going to pull it out on you." He said other things as he became more forceful with his touching, but I didn't hear anything. I felt like my spirit leave my body as I gave him what he wanted.

Afterward, I was left to clean myself up and find my way back to the gymnasium. I was numb as I thought about all that had happened to me over the summer and up to that evening.

I tried to go about my school life as normal, pretending to be like all the other girls. I worked hard to be like I had been before I was "dirty." Determined to find some sort of self-worth, I focused on my schoolwork. But as the weeks progressed, I found myself extremely tired, and it became harder to concentrate on anything. All I wanted to do was sleep.

It wasn't long before I noticed that my jeans weren't fitting right. It was as if they had shrunk. I could hardly get them zipped up. I would barely eat any food, trying to lose the weight that I seemed to be gaining. When I would get home from school, I would quickly close myself in my bedroom. When asked if I was going to join everyone to eat dinner, I would just say that I had eaten a lot at school and had too much homework and that I would get something to eat later.

As the afternoons crawled into the evenings, the trumpet announcing the beginning of Little House on the Prairie's theme song would tell me my family was in the living room. That's when I would peek out my bedroom door to see if I could sneak unnoticed into kitchen to find a little something to calm the rumble in my tummy.

Back to the manual

When I read these scenarios in the training manual, it stirred up all those emotions I had felt but never articulated. I was desperate for answers back then but had no one to ask. The only adult influence I had was my dad. Mom worked, and when she was home she did not talk much. I cannot even remember having a conversation with her. Mom never shared with me her own ideas or dreams.

As I read how pregnancy centers were to provide the client with a mentor who is rooted in compassion of Christ, I naturally asked myself what would my life look like if I'd had this type of support? What would it have meant to me to have had a person to talk with who would not judge me for the situation that I was in or for my family background?

Reading on, I learned that to be a mentor you needed to be trained to listen and to understand the heart. This meant not listening to respond. Given the training I'd already participated in, this concept wasn't new for me. But hearing this guidance in a context that stirred the memories of my youth gave me a totally different perspective on listening to hear the heart. I hadn't been given that opportunity of someone listening to my heart. I hadn't even really known how to explore what my heart was feeling. When an emotion was ever felt, I would shut it down, telling myself it didn't matter.

Understanding more about the client, the guide stated that generally she had no one to talk with or to walk alongside her. As I began to identify with *her*, a passion for the ministry grew inside of me. And I felt more driven to become involved.

CHAPTER 2

Unconditional Love

The main goal of pregnancy centers is to serve all individuals with genuine humility.

This may come as a surprise to some readers, but our primary responsibility is to care for the *person* who walks through the doors. The goal is to understand clients' concerns and why they find themselves there at the center. It is important for the mentor to cultivate a relationship with the person and not make her (or him) just a statistic. The mentor must help the client understand that her own value and her worth are based on truth and not on what others say about her or even on what she is going through.

The more the mentor becomes a safe person for the client to trust, the more open the client is to continue with the educational program—to learning how to take care of herself and her baby or child.

Most people who walk through the doors of a pregnancy center have never experienced unconditional love or even have compassion toward themselves. And in some cases, they've been explicitly told they are not wanted and not valued or that they've messed up; too bad, there is no hope.

Clients may even hear destructive words echo inside their own heads every time they try to make a change in their situation: *What's the use? Things will never change for me. I don't get to dream of something better because I am not smart enough to achieve my dreams. No one cares for me. I am in this alone.*

The guide continues to explain that the client has three basic questions running through her mind: "Will I be judged?" "Do they care enough about my specific situation to listen to me?" "Can they help?"

Mentors are trained to learn empathy. Empathy includes more than sympathy; it requires understanding what the client may be thinking. This kind of understanding is necessary for mentors to function on a level that enables them to observe and analyze the clients' *situation* (not the clients personally) and to offer appropriate assistance. It is also necessary to operate on this level in order to understand the clients' feelings. Mentors are also trained to be watchful of the clients' body language, as well as paying attention to what they're saying. This helps mentors understand what is really being said.

As I continued to read, my thoughts wandered back to my past, and I asked myself, *Did my body language cry out for help?* I know that I kept myself secluded, but did anyone else notice? Was there anyone in my life back then who took enough interest in me to even ask about my well-being? I know I felt guilt and shame. I was confused, filled with destructive self-talk, and depressed. The more I was excluded, the more I felt depressed. Even suicidal thoughts crossed my mind.

Wishing I was invisible

I walked around for weeks with the secret. I didn't tell anybody what had happened to me, let alone confessing that I hadn't had my period in months.

I would often reason with myself that there was no way I

could be pregnant. I knew of other girls who were open about having sex, but I'd never overheard them discuss being in any kind of situation like I thought I might be in.

Given that I rarely had much one-on-one time with my mom, I was a little surprised when she walked into my room. The sun was shining brightly through the window as I was sitting on my bed reading.

Mom casually walked in and went directly to my closet and looked inside where I kept my "female things." As she did this, she asked, "Georgia, why haven't I needed to buy you more supplies?" And before I could answer that question, she sat down on my bed asked me another. "Are you pregnant?"

My answer scared me, yet at the same time, I felt relieved. "I don't know."

Mom didn't say anything after that. She just walked out of the room and went to the kitchen to talk to my dad. It wasn't long after that that I was making a trip to the local health care provider. I didn't even know what was involved in finding out if I was pregnant.

Once we got to the office, the physician quietly took my parents aside as the nurse instructed me as to what she needed from me.

After a short time, we were all led to the doctor's study to have a discussion of what my options were. However, none of the conversation was directed to me. I basically sat behind my parents, and everyone in the room talked about me as if I wasn't even there.

I assume the three of them planned for me to finish the last few weeks of school independently in a basement of a church. To this day, I don't know why I couldn't have just done my schoolwork in the privacy of my own bedroom. But these were the arrangements that were made.

I was dropped off Monday through Friday at a brick building downtown and was told that I had to enter through the back basement doors. The walk down that dark hallway was eerie for me, and it smelled musty. Inside the classroom, there were only a couple of small windows. The florescent lights made the room feel terribly cold and uninviting. I was directed to my desk, which sat facing a corner. When I realized I wasn't the only student in the room, I was hopeful that I would make new friends. There were three (or maybe four) other pregnant girls there. They looked as nervous as I did. It wasn't long into my first day, though, that I could sense these other girls were significantly impaired intellectually. Maybe that was why I was never permitted to talk with them.

I wasn't sure why I couldn't address the teacher (nun) to ask any question. So, I sat facing the corner four hours a day, having no interaction with anyone. Once I had my assignments done, I was left to my own thoughts and questions.

This was when I began to believe many ugly things about myself. I started to think that I was not worthy to be around others and that I was not important enough to have a voice or an opinion. I also thought that I was not smart enough to ask questions. I assumed I was in this situation all by myself and it was what I deserved for being bad.

I looked forward to being done with my studies. And when I left that church for the last time, I told myself that I never wanted to be at that place again (a cold, ugly church with cold, judgmental people).

I always felt that I was pretty much a loner, but I felt even more alone as the days progressed. With every visit at the health care facility, I became more and more self-conscious of the condition of my body. The whispers and remarks that were made in the waiting room made me want to hide. I pretended not to hear what the others were saying to each other or to the office secretary. "Oh, isn't that just a shame," someone would say to someone else, and together, they would shake their heads, looking at me with disapproval written across their faces. It got to the point that I didn't want to go inside to wait for the nurses to call me back. I wished I were invisible. I asked if I could just sit out in the car until it was my turn. I was so depressed that, during this—the only time I got out to socialize with others—all I wanted to do was hide under the car seat.

That was the same summer my most favorite great-uncle was due to come into town, and I was so excited to see him. I always felt special around him. He would call me his "little princess."

All my brothers and my dad were busy cleaning the yard and the brush out from the creek that ran down around the house. My dad had gathered some good-sized rocks and placed them strategically in the creek to create a lovely babbling brook. It was so peaceful to listen to the water gently flow over those rocks.

Once the weeds were mowed down, Dad had placed a couple of picnic tables in the area. It looked like a park, and I was looking forward to the picnic that was being planned.

However, a few days before the arrival of our guests, I was told that I would have to leave and go somewhere else for the day. My dad said, "It will just be too hard to explain the situation that you are in to your great-uncle, and it would just break his heart to see you like this. We will just tell him that you are out visiting colleges and that you wish you could see him but the trip was already planned."

Not being able to see the one person who made me feel like I was special during a time that I felt so alone was devastating to me. Yet I pretended that it was no big deal and that I understood why I was being sent away. But really I didn't understand. I didn't know why I was being punished for doing everything that I had been instructed to do up to this point in my life. And to tell you the truth, I had a lot of questions why.

Why was I born a girl? My parents had named me after my uncle who was fighting in the war, so obviously they had wanted a boy.

Why couldn't I just have been a boy?

Why did being female mean I had no voice, no say? Why did that dictate that my sole purpose was to serve?

Why did a woman have to do as instructed? Why couldn't she just be her own person?

CHAPTER 3

So What Do Pregnancy Centers Offer?

I learned that all services pregnancy centers provide are free, though I didn't know what the ministry had to offer. Of course, one of the centers' obvious services is pregnancy testing. And yes, this is probably the primary reason a client walks through the doors. But as you continue to read you will learn, as I did, that so much more is offered.

Note that some pregnancy centers use the self-testing model of pregnancy test administration, and some are medically staffed. Whether or not the ministry is a medical facility will determine the procedures it uses. To be clear about my training at the ministry I was involved in, it was not medically staffed.

I learned the procedure for the new client seeking a pregnancy test. The client is taken to a private room, where information is taken; this was a good way to get to know the client better and gain an understanding of her background and circumstances. Pregnancy centers follow guidelines found in the privacy act, so the client can be assured that all information is kept confidential. Barring a court ordered or a circumstance where it is believed a client is in some sort of danger (self-afflicted or at the hands of another person), nothing a client shares is disclosed.

As the client waits for the results of the pregnancy test, she is given statistics about sexually transmitted diseases. Then once the test results are done, the client learns the truth about the question that has been secretly haunting her. Sometimes she is excited to find out that she is, in fact, pregnant. However, there are some clients who are not so excited. Whatever emotion the client feels, a mentor is never to rush her. This might mean that she cries without saying a word. We mentors are to give her that time. She has many things going through her head. When she is ready, she will begin to talk.

Mentors are there to help the client. Each situation is different, and we treat all of our clients and their individual situations with respect, valuing them each. Seeing the clients through the Lord's eyes (with unconditional love) we let them know the options that are available. This means being truthful without giving our own personal opinions.

I learned in my training that, most often, the client will not decide about her pregnancy independently and will want to talk with those individuals who are close to her. The mentor is trained to help the client identify all who will be supportive in this journey. The mentor also explains that the center is there to walk alongside her as well.

However, if a woman fears abandonment by the significant people in her life, she may want to choose an abortion. Pregnancy center mentors are trained to listen to her reasons *without judgments, without lecturing, and without talking in a manipulative matter.* The client is told the truth about abortion procedures and the risks involved. Information is also shared with the client about the option of adoption. If the client is interested, the mentor will give her the contact information of a Christian-based organization so that she can make an appointment to meet with a counselor, who can answer questions the client may have.

If the client is still thinking of terminating the pregnancy, she is then asked one question: Would she agree to have an ultrasound (done by a certified technician)? The hope is to show the client that life begins at conception and that she is carrying life within her.

We pray that the client will carry her baby full-term, but if we are told she is choosing differently, we continue to intercede for the mother and unborn child. We never reject or condemn the client. In fact, some centers do follow-up calls, letting the clients know they are more than welcome to talk with someone.

Not certain we will see the client again, we reiterate that if she should need someone to talk with, she and/or the father is always welcome back.

The first visit is usually the longest, but if the client chooses to continue with what we have to offer, the next appointment is made.

What is Earn While You Learn (EWYL)?

I was surprised when the Earn While You Learn (EWYL) curriculum was explained to me. And it is usually a surprise for the client as well. Only being introduced to the ministry because of a missed period, most clients do not understand the scope of the services it offers. Once they understand there are ways to get the much-needed items they worry about being able to provide before the baby is born, some of their anxieties are put at ease.

The program allows clients to receive "mommy or baby bucks" after each private (hour-long) class they attend. They can use those bucks to shop at the store/boutique.

Note that most pregnancy centers have EWYL programs. However, programs at various centers may have different names. Similarly, the point system may be slightly different. Whatever the case, the basic principle remains the same. Clients can obtain "baby bucks" or "points" for arriving on time, having their homework done, and bringing their support person to the center.

The lessons are provided

As eager as I was to get started, I was surprised at how uneasy I felt preparing to meet my first client solo. It was very comforting for me to know that I was guided on which lesson to start with. The client meets one-on-one with a mentor; this ensures that each class offered to the client is specific to his or her needs.

The client has many resources to choose from, covering several areas of interest or need. These include prenatal care (the importance of physical and emotional health for both mom and baby), labor and delivery, infant development and care, parenting and/or life skills, and even Bible studies. There is even a curriculum for the men (dads) specifically. The needs of the client will determine what lesson the mentor will start with. Generally, the precise way this program works at each center is decided by the director of client services at the center. Again, the ministry is not one size fits all, and it is really client focused.

I most enjoy the section discussion called "Understanding Your Baby's Development." Oh my goodness, it is the most amazing and rewarding area (for me) to cover with a client. For a mom-to-be, understanding what is going on inside her body and how her baby is growing is comforting. The unknown is terribly frightening.

Another reason that I have such a desire for this ministry is that these centers educate the pregnant mother on every aspect of the pregnancy up to labor and delivery. Centers even offer lessons on coaching!

I was clueless

As I finished my studies in the corner of a classroom in a church basement, not allowed to make conversation with the other girls or address the nun, she was busy teaching the class on something I wasn't privy to.

What was she teaching? I believe she was teaching the other girls what to expect when in labor. I recall seeing a rather large flip book of sorts with pictures of a baby going down the birth canal. When I tried to glance over my shoulder to see what was being shown, I was sternly told to tend to my own studies and not worry about what was going on.

I truly felt embarrassed for looking over my shoulder; the harshness in her voice made me feel as if I had invaded someone's privacy. I also felt like I was being punished for being in the situation that I was in. Fighting back my tears, I told myself that it just wasn't time for me to worry about such things and that someone would surely clue me in as to what would happen at the appropriate time.

Of course, once I was done with the few short weeks left of school, I never walked into that classroom again. I went about the rest of the summer in deeper and deeper denial. Whenever I showered, I would not look at my body. When I put lotion on myself, I blocked out the fact that my stomach was growing and tried not to wonder if the baby growing inside of me was a girl or boy. Sometimes the baby's movement was scary for me! I just couldn't believe that this sort of movement was normal.

I didn't have too much to say about what I could or could not do during that summer, but I did make one decision that went against my father's wishes. I was very firm in my choice. Consulting with a health care professional, I determined that placing my baby for adoption would be the best decision, and I took it.

It was the only time I believe that I ever had a voice. My dad wanted me to keep the baby so that my parents could raise him or her as one of my siblings. But I knew the heartache of being a child in that household.

Often we kids were told by extended family that we were a burden for our parents. There were many long nights when we would gather around the kitchen table as Dad verbalized his frustration. At times, when his emotions were fully engaged, glasses (or other items) would be thrown through the air, shattering into pieces once they hit whatever solid surface stood in their trajectory.

It was very discouraging to see my parents so frustrated with life—to see how greatly they struggled. The more I witnessed such defeat, the more I wanted things to be different for me.

So, no, I didn't want my baby to be brought up in that type of environment. Besides, I knew how much my parents struggled to keep us six kids clothed and fed. I knew they couldn't handle another.

There were not many pictures taken of me that summer. If pictures were taken, it was from the shoulders up (to my knowledge anyhow) so that there would be no evidence that I had even experienced this pregnancy.

Then the night came when I could not sleep. I experienced some cramping, but it wasn't that big of a deal. I was outside looking for my pet bunny, who had escaped her cage. However, as the pain seemed to linger in time and the discomfort grew more uncomfortable, I thought I should say something to my mom.

Before I knew it, I was being wheeled into the hospital. With each increasingly intense pain I experienced, I became more terrified—to the point of hysterical screaming and crying.

That was when one of the physicians came into the room

and got real close to my face. *"Why don't you just grow up!"* he snapped. *"Shut up and stop your screaming."*

That was when I turned off my emotions (again). I stopped crying. In that moment, I vowed inside my head that I would never let another person see me cry, proving to everyone that I was *"grown-up."*

It is almost eerie thinking back on this moment; it is as if I stopped living, as if everything went quiet.

I must have become unconscious because I don't remember pushing. I only assume my body did what it was designed to do. In and out of consciousness, I saw the health care providers rushing around me. And when I looked down between my legs, I was scared to see the blood-soaked bedding I was lying on.

I didn't find out till years later that my mom had left the hospital. She didn't know that the health care professionals were frantically trying to control my hemorrhaging. Not until she received a phone call back at the house did she know I was in trouble. *"We don't know what else to do for her,"* the caller said, urging her to return to the hospital. *"You just need to get back here."*

My recovery period was very lonely. I was the only one there at the time, and I could hear my baby cry. I asked to hold her, but I was not allowed to do so. I kept asking what was wrong with her and saying I wanted to go see her, but again I was denied.

I had no one to talk to. I had only the many thoughts that ran through my head to keep me company. I wasn't sure how to feel. I felt empty, sad, and in some way left out again. I wasn't sure why I was left alone in the hospital room by myself. I didn't have any visitors. Maybe it was because I would often cry. Or maybe it was because the nurses were tired of me asking to hold my baby. Whatever the reason, the nurses eventually had

Georgia Barnes

me moved to another floor. I told myself that I wasn't important enough to have someone help me sort out how I was feeling. I was devastated and all alone.

♥ ♥ ♥

It is hard for me to remember something that I had stuffed so deep and for so long. Yet as I was going through the training, I became aware that God was still healing my heart. I know now that it is okay if I don't remember everything about my first pregnancy. I also realize that the fact that I still sometimes cry doesn't mean that I will always cry. Truthfully, it comes back to me in pieces; memories surface still till this day. Once I evaluate what I was remembering, I ask for God to give me truth in those moments—thus not denying the difficult memory that surfaced happened but not allowing it to destroy me either.

CHAPTER 4

It's All about Relationships

Pregnancy centers are not about getting the client through a lesson. What is important is building bonds with our clients. It is unfortunate that most (not all) clients that come to the center do not have a family or network of people who provide them with practical or emotional support. So in a sense, we become our clients' family.

Mentors understand that they are colaboring with Jesus to build that relationship. In some cases, we become the first person that has shown the client unconditional love—the first person who will, ultimately, become someone she can trust.

Accepting the individual is a vital part of showing unconditional love, even if the client is making decisions that would go against what 'we' would do in her place.

True humility is a characteristic that mentors must have. Humility is not making yourself out to be a know-it-all. Rather, it fosters a desire to truly assist the other person. To volunteer is to see the client through the eyes of Jesus, to be willing to serve the client at her point of need, and to never force one's own personal agenda on the client.

Identifying emotions

Most of us in general are not even aware of our emotions. We are just trying to get through each day and really do not pay much attention of *how* we are feeling. Yet, even though we are not aware what we are feeling, when we are facing difficulties in our lives, our reactions make it evident to others that we are struggling through something. Some of us aren't *responding* to people and circumstances; we are *reacting*. There is a difference. I know because I was that person who would react.

As mentors, we don't call ourselves counselors or therapists. This is made clear to the client; we are not professionals. However, we are trained to identify the emotion that each client is experiencing and help the client see it. Through this training, along with guidance from the Lord, we can help clients sort what they are truly feeling. A method that generally helps clients see what is going on inside them more clearly is to repeat a client's statements, allowing her to hear her own words out loud.

"What I hear you saying is that …" "I think you are saying that …"

In some cases, a client may realize she is speaking harshly about the situation and work through the emotions on their own, just by talking it out.

There are many different types of emotions, but what I have noticed is that, rather than explore our emotions, we (all people) generally sum them up into two categories—happy (joyful) or mad (angry). If it doesn't feel good, I am angry. If it feels good, I must be happy. There are other feelings than just these two. For instance, I knew a person who would equate the feeling of disappointed with anger. Feeling angry and feeling disappointed are not the same.

I mentored one client who had strong feelings of anger, resentment, and guilt. It was heartbreaking for me to listen to her weekly struggles. This single mom was truly exhausted. One day, she said to me, "It is not fair. I am judged because I am not able to be home to 'nurture' my children. Yet I am judged if I am not able to provide just the basics for them. I am judged if I don't take my child to the doctor every time he is sick. Yet I get points (and eventually get fired) for not showing up to work to take my child to the doctor. I can't win!"

Truthfully, it was hard for me to hear her frustration. I only had one answer to her many burdens—give it to God. But she didn't want to hear that from me in the moment. So I just sat there and listened, taking mental notes of what her heart was saying.

After she was done, I validated her feelings by assuring her that I understood the pressure she felt. Then I asked if we could offer her heavy load to God in prayer. I told her that, when I pray, I believe that Father God hears and sends help in all our circumstances.

What excites me most is when a client like this one comes back the following week and shares with me how God has provided. I get so excited when He does that! As each client tells me how Father God has provided, I see hope returning to their eyes—and that hope fills me with joy.

These types of ministries provide a safe environment for clients to share their emotions of frustration and bitterness, without fear that their words will be taken the wrong way or used against them. We just love and value each client.

> I heard one person say that people today are just hard-hearted and do not feel emotions. I don't think this is true. I believe what is true for many people who appear emotionless is that their hearts are calloused. But a calloused heart does not mean a lack of emotions. It simply means that

it is more difficult for the person to acknowledge these emotions and to deal with them.

One day, I was out running on the side of some country roads and a young person drove past me without so much as moving the line they were driving. The road was not busy. In fact, that car was the only one on the road. It was as if this person could have cared less whether or not they had hit me. I instantly asked why they did not care or value me. And I heard the Lord say, "It's not that they don't value your life. It's that they don't value their own life." That was eye-opening for me—it helped me understand that the way people react or respond has a lot to do with how they are feeling inside about themselves.

I want to reiterate that mentors show love and value each client (and the client's family) as Christ loves and values each of us. We provide information, support, and spiritual direction. We cannot change the clients or rescue them—only God can do that. But knowing someone is there for them brings clients comfort.

I believe God sang over each of us when we were being knitted together in our mothers' wombs. And that unique song is being sung consistently throughout our lives. When a client can begin to believe this; that the Lord is singing over her, she realizes that God is signing over her baby too.

Confiding in the empty pages

If I'd had a pregnancy center to go to, I would have gotten help identifying my emotions. As I had no church family to reach out to, my parents were the only adult guidance that I had. My mom worked many long, hard hours, so I didn't have her around much. I didn't really have anyone to help me through what was going on with me. No one was there to guide me through the emotions I was feeling—either during my pregnancy or after I had given birth.

All kinds of feelings and questions that ran through my thoughts. The day I came home from the hospital after having given birth to my baby girl, I seriously felt like I was in the Twilight Zone. I felt my head spinning as I walked up the stairs. Members of my family were talking to me, but it was as it they were far away. I could not understand what they were saying to me.

I didn't know how I should feel. I knew that I felt empty, but was I supposed to feel that way? Yes, I had chosen to place my baby up for adoption, but that didn't mean I didn't feel sad. Unable to explain how I felt, I chose not to say anything to anyone.

When my body did as it was designed to do (produce milk), I wasn't even aware that was something to expect. One day when I was walking into the kitchen, my dad called my brothers into the room to point it out. "See," he told them, "this is what breasts are designed for."

I was in total shock that my father would call it out like that to my brothers, rather than discreetly telling me to change my blouse or go look in a mirror. Anything would have been better than what he did. I pretty much stayed in my bedroom after that.

I didn't get to start school that fall when everyone else did. I only had to wait a few more weeks, but the wait felt endless. Once my brothers went back to school, there weren't any noises in the house. Again, I was left alone with my tormenting thoughts. Without the noises of my brothers squabbling, the only thing I could hear was destructive words I believed about myself—and it got louder each day.

The one thing that broke the silence in my day would be

my father talking on his CB radio. But even that became a far-off sound because the ugly things I thought about myself consumed me. My mind-set pushed me to feel extreme sadness and worthlessness. I truly could not understand why I had even been born.

Not wanting anyone see me cry and tell me that I wasn't "grown-up," I would hide myself to privately cry. Often, I would be curled up on the floor on the other side of my bed (so no one who happened to walk into my room would see me) in a puddle of tears.

Those six weeks felt as if they were months. If I wasn't struggling to keep my blouses dry, I was desperately trying to get back into my favorite pair of Calvin Klein jeans.

Those rare times I decide to be with the family to watch The Greatest American Hero, I would have to hide my eyes whenever a commercial for baby powder would air—or any baby scene for that matter. It would only remind me of when I'd heard my baby girl cry in the hospital. That same aching desire I'd had to hold her would well up inside me, and once more, I would find myself asking, Why couldn't I have held her once or even seen her? The question would be followed by a series of what-ifs—the primary one being, what if I had acted on my notion to take her and run away from the hospital? That would lead to me to calling myself a coward for not having done it.

This kind of mental dialogue led a small part of me to think I would have been better off running away with her. That couldn't have been any worse than the struggle I was in. I had a well of grief but no idea how to handle it.

As hard it was to be home, returning to high school was even harder. I wanted things to be like before this all this had happened to me. But I didn't know who I was before. I was only programed to perform a certain way. I didn't remember ever having a good thought about myself before my "knight" came into my life and told me wonderful things about me. But those had all been lies. In his last letter, he had told me he was just having fun with me, "a kid."

Somehow, the word got out that I had gotten pregnant on the night my heart was broken in the parking lot. My peers would look at me with disgust as they walked past me and make accusations that I had given birth to an inbred child—saying cruelly that it had to have been someone from my family who had impregnated me, as no one in his right mind would find me attractive enough to even touch me. It was also the common consensus that I was an awful mom to have given up my baby. "What kind of mom are you, anyway, placing your baby up for adoption?! You don't even desire to be a mother."

No one at school thought I had the right to be there. I was scum. I was even told, when I went in search of help with what classes I should be taking in preparation for college, "Girls like you don't go on to college. In fact, you will just be lucky to graduate."

I tried to let all those words being said about me roll off my back and pretended (again) I didn't hear or care what others said about me. But deep inside of me, all of this negativity tore at my soul. It destroyed what little self-esteem I'd tried to muster up to walk down the halls at school in the first place.

As the weeks passed, I secretly wrote my grief and sadness, along with the self-hatred I felt in a journal that I hid between my mattress and box springs. It was my safe place, where I could let out my feelings.

However, one day when I came home from school, my parents confronted me about what I had written. I felt so violated that my own private words were exposed that I went out to the burn barrel and ripped each page out and burned them one by one. I felt devastated as I was doing it, like I was betraying myself in some sort of way. I wasn't just destroying pages from a journal; I was destroying a part of my life, a part of me.

So, I know about self-hatred. I know about reacting, rather than responding in life. And this didn't get any better as the years went by and I was married and with young children.

♥♥♥

Note that I do not begrudge what my parents did or did not do during my childhood. I truly believe that they did what they thought best for me. My father has since passed away. However, years before his death, I was able to forgive him. I could do this by asking myself a few questions:

What kind of upbringing did he have as a child?

Was he ever told he was a burden?

What things did he witness as a young boy?

Did he know that God created everyone, including him, for a glorious purpose?

Asking myself these questions and others like them enabled me to find compassion for him.

And one thing is sure; he may have had his shortcomings as a father, but he was one heck of a grandfather to my children. I like to believe that he encounter God's unconditional love and that changed him into the man my children loved. Whatever or however it happened, I know in my heart that he was a new person.

CHAPTER 5

What Type of Lessons Do Centers Offer?

As I mentioned earlier, each client (male or female) can receive "baby bucks" when they participate in lessons by way of a program called Earn While You Lean (EWYL). Pregnancy centers are equipped with many resources, and all are made available to clients for free! I want to explain briefly what it is that a person can glean from going to these types of ministries. In fact, even though I will be there to help my own children if or when they decide to have children of their own, I will encourage them to sign up for classes at their local pregnancy center. I believe everyone benefits when a parent has a better understanding of every aspect of baby / child development (inside and outside the womb).

Parenting

The lessons vary from infant care to parenting an adolescent. Clients are taught what milestones to look for and how to understand the emotional needs (and sometimes demands) that a child has at each age level or stage. The curriculum even covers exercises to help children develop their five senses, to stimulate brain activity (that is age appropriate), and to emphasize the importance of playtime. This reassures parents that they aren't doing anything wrong and that their child is normal.

Teaching parents how to communicate with and love their children is so vital to building a strong relationship. The lessons are based on child psychology and biblical principles. There are many things to glean from these lessons. I often encourage all parents to plug into their local pregnancy centers, even if they don't need the material assistance.

I didn't know how to be a mom

I had been told I was the "worst mom ever" and that I didn't deserve to be a mother. Those words haunted me. So when I became a mom, I wanted everything to be perfect. I was so uncertain about every aspect of caring for my babies that it seriously took me all day to do the simplest tasks. I didn't know what to expect and looked forward to their wellness checkups so that I could ask the doctor my list of questions. Even then, I would often call the nurse at the office—sometimes two or three times a day—between checkups with the doctor. I was certain that I had become what the voices from my past that echoed in my head each day had predicted—the worst mom ever.

Given that I didn't get any nurturing when I was young (none that I could remember anyhow) I didn't know how to interact with my own children. I thought being a good mom was about making sure children had nice, clean clothes that fit them properly and ensuring they had consistent schedules that included mealtimes, learning times, and bedtime. I thought that's what it meant to nurture my children. Playtime was hard for me to incorporate because I really didn't know how to do it. I had a distorted belief about playing because of things that had been told to me when I was young—"You are a burden to your parents." "You need to learn to be more responsible."

I figured if I got my children the toys, they would know how to play with them.

♥ ♥ ♥

I wasn't much help to my children when it came to identifying and working through their emotions because, quite honestly, I didn't know how to work through my own. I had so much negative self-talk going on inside my head that I was constantly trying to prove to everyone (and myself) that I was a "good" mother. And thus, I really didn't talk with anyone.

♥ ♥ ♥

A friend recently told me that people thought I was a snob because, when they tried to talk with me, I never engaged them in conversation. That shocked me. I am far from being snobby. And her revelation only revealed to me that my internal dialogue must have consumed my every thought. I truly was a lonely person.

♥ ♥ ♥

Throwing birthday parties would stress me out. I hadn't had experiences like birthday parties being thrown for me during my childhood, so I was clueless on how to celebrate. Whenever my kids would get invited to a birthday party, I would end up feeling like a failure. Comparing what I did to what other moms did for such celebrations only confirmed that I was, indeed, "the worst mom ever."

♥ ♥ ♥

If only I had a known about pregnancy centers that taught parenting classes for free, I might have been able to enjoy my time with my children, instead of trying to prove I was a "good mom."

I would have felt so much more secure in my role as a mom, and as a result, I would have been able to better connect emotionally with them.

Understanding children's need for interaction would have helped me better prioritize my day. Instead of the insane schedule of cleaning and taking care of the lawn I undertook, I would have been more relaxed and more able to celebrate with them as they discovered the world around them.

❤ ❤ ❤

For years, I felt horrible over the mistakes that I felt I had made as a young mom. Then one day, I sensed the Lord say to me, "Georgia, I know your heart. You love your children. You did not intentionally hurt your children." That is when I gave this issue to the Lord and asked Him to heal those unintentional wounds that I had caused. And I trust that He will.

Sharing the Gospel/Bible studies

Just like parenting classes, the Bible studies lessons will take the client from being an infant in understanding biblical truths to eating solid food, so to speak. These lessons reveal who God is and the great love God has for everyone. The lessons help clients see who they are—giving them access to scripture that shows God created them for a great purpose and that their lives have value. This is liberating for clients, who typically define themselves by the situations they find themselves in. In most cases, clients have a bad opinion of church or those who go to church, because, at church, they were judged or felt as if they were being judged.

I never grew up in church. My family would attend Christmas service or go to church on Easter Sunday; I even played handbells for those special events. Baby Jesus was born on Christmas in a manger, and on Easter he rose from the tomb—that was pretty much all there was to my religion.

But when I was about twenty years old, I wanted to know if church had something for me. I would put on the only dress I owned, the one I'd made when I was in high school. It was a sundress that tied on top of my bare shoulders. It wasn't very conservative, but it was a dress. It didn't matter what church I walked into, I would get the same reaction. I can still recall the gasps I got from the women and the glances I got from the men. They all were aware of me being there, but not one greeted me. So I understand having a bad opinion of people who go to church and feeling judged. The sad thing about it was that I thought that these people had a link with God, so He must have told them I was bad.

The Bible studies offered at the pregnancy centers are designed to teach truths, not give clients more dos and don'ts that will only frustrate them and put more demands on them. And if a client is interested in finding a church, a list is usually given, providing service times and information about any transportation or child care a church may offer.

Note that pregnancy centers encourage clients to find a church family (support) that is Christ-centered (based on unconditional love and nonjudgmental). However, clients are never made to feel guilty if they choose not to go to church. It is truly in God's timing, and all we are to do is love our clients unconditionally.

Male mentoring: Fatherhood 24-7

Men whose hearts call them to teach the fatherless to be fathers are priceless to the ministry. Male mentors lead men from every walk of life. Unfortunately, there are a lot of young men who feel angry, afraid, and even ashamed about becoming a father. Often this is simply a result of them not having had a good relationship with their own dads (if they had any relationship with their fathers at all).

The goal of the ministry is not to overpower these men but to empower them—leading them through a biblically based curriculum, teaching them of the father in heaven, and explaining God's design for family. These fathers and fathers-to-be need to feel safe to share their thoughts and feelings about being a man in today's world and the pressures involved. I believe that, deep inside, these men really do want to be good fathers and to support their families. But how does one break out of the vicious cycle of being fatherless? Our male mentors are willing to give of their time in order to come alongside these men, showing them how to be the fathers they themselves never had.

I would like to mention that not all the men who come into the center are fatherless. They might just need a support person to talk to and to get good godly advice. My heart grows so huge when I see this type of mentorship growing between the two generations. Most of these men want to raise their families in a way that is honorable. Seriously think about it; if we can change the understanding of one man (father)—if we can help him truly see himself as God sees him—then his whole family will change. One family at a time can change a community, with a ripple effect that will change the world.

Life skills

The lessons in this series teach clients important skills, like how to create a résumé, how to have a successful interview, and how to budget and balance a bank statement. Other skills taught include how to shop for a vehicle and vehicle insurance and how to plan meals and make grocery lists.

All these lessons teach communication skills, decision-making skills, how to set realistic goals, how to respect others, and how to function as a unified family. Like I have said, pregnancy centers equip families with the skills to thrive, not just survive. Contrary to what some people think, pregnancy centers are not about giving people handouts. Rather, they're about helping people become more successful.

Abstinence education

Another area of service that pregnancy centers do for free is abstinence education. We occasionally get invited to come into schools and explain to the young people that everyone is valuable for who he or she is and not what he or she does.

Abstinence is the only 100 percent effective means of preventing all sexually transmitted diseases, unwanted pregnancy, and the emotional consequences often associated with sex outside of marriage.

I know about basing my worth on performing. The beliefs I had for many years told me I had no rights and I that I had been placed on this earth to serve in every area of my life. When I was asked to do something, I only heard demands. I didn't believe that I had a choice. I didn't believe that I could say no.

I was an emotional mess, and it took years of mentoring to show me that my value was in just being me. I was taught that I didn't have to perform to be accepted and loved by God. This led me to understand I didn't need to perform to be accepted and loved by others. This lesson has been very liberating for me and has enabled me to truly feel comfortable being me.

CHAPTER 6

The Misunderstanding
about the Ministry

As I served as a mentor at the center, I always felt that I was the one being blessed. It was a healing journey for me to mentor others. It is hard for us to understand, but sometimes we can get the most healing when we give our time to others.

To my great surprise I was offered a job. And boy did the Lord stretch me a lot. One of the main tasks that I handled was going out into the community to secure donations for our annual banquet and silent auction. Going around to different business to ask for donations was a bit intimidating. But once I stepped out, I grew to love it. I was, however, surprised to learn that most people I encountered really had no idea what we did at the center or even what the ministry was about, even though the center had been a part of the community for over twenty years.

I met people with all sorts of opinions about the ministry, some favorable, some not so favorable. I would simply introduce myself as an employee of the center and ask if whoever I was speaking to would like to know about some of the services that we offered.

Here are some of responses I would get:

"Care to hear about pregnancy centers? I really don't care."

"I am beyond childbearing years, so I don't really need to know what services the center offers."

"Isn't that just for young girls who find themselves in trouble?"

"Isn't that just a pro-life thing?"

"Oh, I am sorry, I don't get involved in politics."

"Don't the centers get enough government funds?"

"I don't have any desire to help out the local pregnancy center. I have a daughter, and both her and her husband work hard. They don't get any 'handouts.'"

Oh my goodness, I would get all sorts of looks as well. I would get mean looks and irritated looks; looks that said, *I don't have time for this*; and looks that asked, *Are you serious?*

Normally, I would go running the other way if someone responded to me like that. But now that it was my job to engage with the public about the center, I didn't do so. I didn't even get upset with these responses; I knew the person I was talking to had no clue what type of ministry the pregnancy center was. The Lord gave me the courage and the words.

I would explain, yes, it is true that you may never need our services, but you might just meet someone or know of someone who could really benefit from our services. That would open the door for me to briefly tell them the things the center does.

When I explained that anyone could come to the center for help and that there wasn't an income requirement to meet, people's attitude changed. This allowed me to share more about what we do.

Once business owners understood what the ministry was about, they were eager to help in different ways. Some area businesses even allowed us to advertise upcoming events by hanging up flyers on their community bulletin boards.

Who is it for?

We get a variety of clients at the center. Single mothers and/or fathers (or couples) who already have their hands full with the children and just need some help come to us. So do parents who work but still don't make enough to get diapers. Really, anyone who just needs a little assistance or simply wants to take the classes is welcomed. After taking an hour-long class, the parent/caregiver will receive baby bucks to shop at the boutique. At first, clients may think this setup is a hassle, but they quickly realize that they are gaining valuable information as they are learning to parent with unconditional love.

We even had a client come in who had thought she was done having babies when, to her surprise, she became pregnant again. She wanted the reassurance that she was well prepared during pregnancy and labor.

"Obviously, I have done this before," this expecting mother said, glancing at her nine-year-old. "But it was so long ago I am not sure I even know what to expect."

We sometimes would get parent(s) who had been ordered by the court to take parenting classes. This is something I think is awesome. We have an opportunity to love these clients, many of whom, up to that point, may have only gotten judgmental looks and or words that destroy.

I know about destroying words: "You are the worst mom ever. You don't deserve to be a mother."

Trust me—harsh, judgmental words destroy a person's self-worth. And to be completely honest, most of these destructive words spoken to clients come from the mouths of their own immediate family members. True or not, we are to have a compassionate heart serving these individuals.

Personally, I didn't need to know the nitty-gritty details about why these clients had to take parenting classes. In my mind-set, our call was to help them see their own value—because, when clients see and understand the value that they themselves have, they will value others (their children).

I will never forget one young couple I had the pleasure of mentoring. We were doing a lesson that taught making eye contact as a way to convey love to your child. It was being explained that making eye contact with your children when talking to them fills their emotional tanks. On the flip side, giving disapproving looks makes the child feel unloved and not valued. As we watched the DVD that went with this lesson, I was watching the body language of the couple. They were truly engaged with the video and were taking notes.

After the lesson was done, I asked if they could remember getting looks of approval and love or rejection and disapproval. The gentleman looked up from his hand and said, "I didn't have either, not even when I was in school. I was made to face the corner."

My heart was so sad to hear this. At that moment, I was overwhelmed with love and compassion. I felt inspired to tell him that he has so much value and that our God in heaven and earth loves him more than he could ever think or imagine. I meant it too! With all my heart, I did.

After that specific lesson, this client opened up more about what he would like to do once he got his children back. Unfortunately, this didn't happen for them at that time, and he was so devastated. I will never forget when this father asked me, "Why do people look at only what we"—he was referring to him and his girlfriend—"have done in the past and not what we doing now?"

I had no answer for him, but my thoughts often go to this couple. I pray that God has sent loving people to come alongside and nurture and love them as Christ would. I will never forget the sadness he had. He was so broken.

At the center, we also supervise court order parent visitations. What I didn't know at the time—most places that offer supervision charge the supervised parent anywhere from fifty to seventy-five and, in some cases, a hundred dollars to supervise these visits. At the center where I worked, supervision was offered for free. The only stipulation was that the supervised parent take parenting classes. What is beautiful about this is the relationship that is built between the mentor and the parent goes beyond the court-ordered time.

As you are reading this, I hope you have come to an understanding that pregnancy centers aren't just about pregnancy testing and pushing a pro-life agenda. These centers are about loving and valuing the individual where he or she is at. They focus on coming alongside these women and men to provide support. We make available a safe place for the client to catch his or her breath. And we provided clients with someone safe to talk to, along with the assurance that what they say won't be manipulated or held over them.

My belief is that most people today are just surviving, just doing what they need to do each day. We (I mean society in general) are so busy trying to make ends meet that we do not know there is greatness inside of each of us. And sometimes our own self-talk (our thoughts) is negative, which leads to a negative attitude that eventually is displayed in our actions.

This isn't the life God has for any of us. No, we are to thrive. But we cannot thrive on our own. We need a community of people around us, to encourage us and to walk alongside us when things get hard.

This is what pregnancy centers do; the mentors at the centers love, encourage, and come alongside of people and always take their circumstances to the Lord (praying for their needs).

I personally don't take prayer lightly. It is not just a cliché to me. I know prayers make a difference. My belief is that prayer is a key to unlock heaven. We are simply asking God to intervene in an individual's situation. I trust and know that He does. Many times, I would have clients tell me how God had answered their/ our prayer. And each time I would be so overwhelmed as I thanked Father God for answering my friends' prayer.

Not only do pregnancy centers provide these services mentioned, but they also help by providing material assistance. Depending on the donations that come in, baby boutiques (stores at the center) can supply diapers, formula, and clothing for a child up to preschool age. Some boutiques even have maternity clothes for mom. There are also hygiene products for the whole family. They even have gently used (and sometimes new) toys.

CHAPTER 7

Where Does the Money Come From?

Unlike what is said or believed by some people, pregnancy centers are in fact nonprofit organizations and are funded by donation. In other words, no government (neither federal nor state) assistance is given. Yet it is amazing how many people these centers can help with the money donated and/or raised.

Nonprofit organizations must have an annual report that accounts for how funds are being used. This allows you to see how the nonprofit you support uses each dollar.

There are several fund-raising opportunities throughout the year. Most pregnancy centers have an annual banquet to raise money for the ministry. This is not the only fund raising pregnancy centers do. In fact, there are several fund-raising events throughout the year, and these can vary from center to center.

Most centers will hold an annual *Baby Bottle Drive (BBD)* as well. If you have not heard of a Baby Bottle Drive, you may not understand what it is that we collect. Hint, it's not baby bottles. We collect change (coins) inside baby bottles. The slogan, "Your change can change lives." If you belong to a church that supports your local pregnancy center, then you are aware that this fund-raiser runs from Mother's Day to Father's Day. However, you may not understand this is not exclusive to churches. No, anyone can request baby bottles to collect change. There are no amount restrictions. You can request as few or as many baby bottles as you think you can fill. Participants can include preschools, day care centers, baby stores, department stores, nail salons, hair salons, tanning salons, tire stores, auto part stores, and on and on. You get the picture. Every baby bottle that is filled makes a huge difference.

There is usually a *Walk for Life (or Families)* to raise funds annually. Anyone can walk; whether you are a client, an employee, a volunteer, a church member, or just someone who wants to get involved, you will be welcome. There is no maximum amount to raise. All proceeds help support the ministry.

Monetary donations are another important part of the centers' budgets. You may choose to support the ministry throughout the year; you can make one-time, monthly, or even weekly donations. For any of these, you will get a receipt for your own records. Trust that every cent goes into the ministry; donations help fund everything from learning materials to baby wipes to the electric bill to copy machine paper. As I have mentioned several times, pregnancy centers are 100 percent donor funded and do not get any assistance from the government.

You could also make *donations to the baby boutique / center store*. Some churches will have a baby shower for their local center. That is always fun. I love to hear how people fund-raise for us. We had one family support us in a unique way. The family asked everyone who came to their family reunion to donate an item for the boutique. One year, we were all speechless when this family brought in new baby seats, diapers, wipes, baby swings, Pack 'n Plays, and baby clothes. Watching this donation come in was truly amazing; they kept going back to their vehicle to bring items into the center, and we were truly humbled by their generosity. We had clients who were very much in need of these items (especially the car seats) and we were deeply grateful.

It always seems to go that way; whenever we have a need, we lift it to the Lord in prayer, and He richly provides every time.

Holiday projects

The center I worked at would send out appeals for help with supplying Thanksgiving dinner or Christmas for the families that we served. This too is something I hold dear to my heart. I have been on the receiving end of those types of charitable acts. It is very difficult to hold back tears when you look in the eyes of these clients with a box full of fixin's for their Thanksgiving dinner. There is a profound sense of gratitude when a client no longer has to try to figure out how to squeeze his or her already tight budget for such extras.

Adopt a Family for Christmas program is another incredible way to love unconditionally those individuals who strive so hard to provide. The ministry where I served would evaluate the different clients that were in our Earn While You Learn program. We would consider many factors, but primarily, we were determining whether or not clients had a network of people (family and friends) who came alongside them to support them (not just financially but also by walking alongside them on their journey of life). If we found the client was struggling alone (which we did in most cases) we would ask the client for permission to put an appeal out on his or her behalf. We never revealed names of either side of this project (those who were giving or those who were receiving).

What tugged at my heartstrings so often is when we asked for a Christmas list; the clients would list the most basic things. The lists wouldn't include elaborate game systems or 'designer' clothes or things of that nature. Rather, parents would ask for gloves and hat for a fast-growing toddler, matchbox cars for an eight-year-old boy, a pink sweatshirt for a ten-year-old girl, and other things like that. It always seemed that when we asked the parents what kind of gifts they would like, they would insist that they did not want anything, just a nice Christmas for their children. Really, what parent doesn't want to have nice things for his or her child under the tree?

I have no words to articulate how much love was felt when we presented the clients with boxes wrapped with colorful wrapping and bright bows. It was such a humbling honor to be the conduit between the giver and the receiver. Truly great things can happen in those last weeks of the year (with a small number of people). It makes one think: What could happen if more people got involved, and not just once but throughout the entire year? I believe great things could be accomplished, more than we can even ask or imagine (Ephesians 3:20).

I personally love adopting a family for Christmas. Growing up with five brothers, I came from a family that didn't have much. We grew most of the food we ate, so I personally would look forward to that basket of holiday fixin's that we would receive from an unknown giver. I especially loved the fresh fruit and nuts. Christmas was hard for my parents. I remember when I was a small girl I secretly hoped that Santa was real because I knew my parents could not afford new gifts for us kids, and I only wanted a Raggedy Ann doll. To my surprise, I had one under the tree. She was beautifully handmade, one of a kind. And to this day, I have her. She is very fragile, and she is in much need of professional mending, but I will place her under my Christmas tree every year. The year I received her, I remember saying to myself, *I can have nice things too.* I hold these types of holiday projects close to my heart—because I want all children to know that they can have nice things as well.

I have since learned that other centers set up ways for clients to earn extra "baby bucks" or "mommy/daddy money" by participating in a study especially designed to explain the reason for the Christmas celebration. The store is filled with new items that have been collected throughout the year, specifically for the Christmas store. Clients have a sense of pride, having earned what they spend in the Christmas store, and they get to pick out their child's gifts themselves. It is just one more way to boost parents' morale. And it was noted that this method enables the center to reach more families, rather than just the few they serve by adopting a whole family. Oh my goodness, I love this ministry!

How can you help?

As my story demonstrates, I could have benefited greatly by going to a pregnancy center back when I was secretly struggling to survive. I was very naive and didn't understand much of what was going on with me or all the different things I was going through. It was not only the physical changes that baffled me, but also the emotional and spiritual changes I was undergoing. I did not know how to identify how I was feeling or even what I was internally thinking. Yet every morning, I pushed to get through another day, not realizing I wasn't really living; I was just going through the motions.

My heart is deeply connected to the ministry because it allows me to be that support person I desperately needed. Truthfully, I think everyone can benefit from having a mentor in his or her life. Having someone to ask those parenting questions and knowing that you will not be judged for asking them is priceless. So too is having a sense of being loved unconditionally; ultimately, this love helps new parents through the journey of being a thriving family. Those who have a good family and/or church network may already have these types of people to walk alongside them. But what about those who don't?

If you are wondering how or if you should get involved, here are a few simple ways to get started.

- Be a prayer partner with your local pregnancy center.
- Be a liaison (contact person) with your church, workplace, and/or community.
- Become a monthly partner; all donations are tax deductible.
- Volunteer as a client mentor or help with various tasks around the center.
- Assist with fund-raisers.
- Donate items for the baby boutique (store).
- Do you like to knit, crochet, or sew? Make blankets.

I encourage you to plan a visit to your local pregnancy center. Take a tour, look at the resources, and talk to the director to see what the needs are for the center in your area. If you have new ideas for fund-raising, share them. Centers are always looking for ways to cultivate awareness for the ministry.

You know, there have been days when I felt down (heavy with my own stuff) before going to mentor, only to find afterward that my heart is soaring. That is why I believe the Lord guided me to volunteer. He knew that me giving my time to help someone else would bless me beyond words. And that, my friend, is a blessing. I promise, once you get involved, you will feel as if you are walking away with more than you gave.

Maybe you are the one needing a little help

It doesn't matter your age or your circumstances, do not be afraid to reach out for help. I assure you, whatever you are going through, it is not a surprise to God, and He can guide you. I want to encourage you to find a pregnancy center near you, make an appointment, or go visit. Contrary to what some may say, staff and volunteers are full of compassion and offer a safe place to talk.

Others may have told you that the pregnancy is a mistake or that you have messed your life up. You might even believe you have a handle on it and you can go at it alone. Trust me, things get too heavy to carry when you go it alone. We aren't meant to do life alone (Ecclesiastes 4:9–10). We need one another to hold us up when things become too heavy. We need others to speak words of truth (biblical) and value when we are only hearing our own words of failure.

You might be a parent already, and you feel you have a handle on parenting, but what do you do on those days you feel like your failing? It would have been helpful for me if I had known about this sort of ministry when I was a young mom. There were many times I wished I had someone to talk with to help me maneuver through those challenging years.

The ministry is free! It is not based on your income, whether or not you have a job, or whether you are a single parent or married. These types of centers do their best to work around each client's schedule (to the best of their ability). In my experience, I have found that the people who serve at these types of centers are the most unconditionally loving people you will ever meet.

You will find people who are willing to invest time in your life and to be an ear to listen to your heart. Most of all, you will find someone who will lift your needs in prayer to Father God.

Care Net–affiliated pregnancy centers are faith based, and while staff members and volunteers are motivated by the love of Jesus Christ, we never impose our faith on those we serve. To find a center near you, go to https://www.care-net.org/find-a-pregnancy-center.

I mentioned Care Net only because this is the affiliation of the clinics I worked and volunteered with. There are also clinics that are associated with Heartbeat International and Life Matters, and I have learned that all these clinics basically minister in the same way.

Those of you who've had abortions

We are all called to walk in a life of freedom, and sometimes chains of our past prevent us from any significant progress. Though I personally may not know what sort of emotional or physical challenges a woman may have if her past choices did involve an abortion, I do know that there is help. Care Net–affiliated pregnancy centers offer nonjudgmental and confidential care to women and men who have grief because of an abortion. For a list of centers that offer these services and to obtain a list of helpful resources and websites, go to https://www.care-net.org/i-had-an-abortion.

PART 2

The Veil of Self-Deception Removed

A Birth Mom's Reunion

CHAPTER 8

Becoming a New Person

For years, deep down inside I hated myself. I thought I had no value and that I was disposable. I even allowed people to treat me that way. I knew that certain people only came around me to get something from me. Yes, secretly I hoped the outcome would play out differently, but each time, the outcome would end up the same—I was tossed out like an old pair of shoes.

When I was told in my twenties I could be a "new person"—that the "old person" would be gone—I jumped at the chance. I really had no understanding of what it meant. But if there was a way to rid of "me" Georgia, I was in.

Unfortunately, when I took the first step of faith, I didn't have anyone to disciple (teach) me, so I ended up with a bunch of legalistic rules. I constantly tried to find the joy that faith was supposed to bring but often found only frustration. I was too busy checking off the dos and don'ts. I didn't understand about having a relationship with my savior.

Desperately seeking worth in my relationships, I often found myself lost even more trying to please everyone. The feeling that I was insignificant and had no worth grew with each failed relationship. I didn't understand what love meant even when my now husband proposed to me. I honestly thought he saw me just like all the others had and would eventually throw me away once he tired of me.

I fought and struggled for many years after that day I prayed to be born again. But finding contentment eluded me. Even with my husband and two beautiful children, I still felt I wasn't good enough. I would put on my happy face before going to church. However, each week I struggled to figure out why I felt so lonely. I knew that my sadness wasn't how Christians were supposed to feel. So I concluded that I just wasn't good enough for God to make me into a new person.

One night, the heaviness of disappointment, regret, and even grief overwhelmed me. I found myself crying. I was tired of pretending to be happy. Sitting on a cement step in our garage, smoking my cigarette and drinking my wine cooler, I told the Lord I didn't want to do life anymore. I said that if He was for real, then He would have to come down and help me. That night was the beginning of my journey with Father God.

Shortly after my desperate prayer, I was blessed with women to help me with my walk of faith. They invested their time in me and began to show me Bible scriptures that explained who I am. One of the first scriptures that gave me great hope is found in Ephesians. It reads:

> For we are His workmanship [His own master work, a work of art], created in Christ Jesus [reborn from above—spiritually transformed, renewed, ready to be used] for good works, which God prepared [for us] beforehand [taking paths which He set], so that we would walk in them [living the good life which He prearranged and made ready for us]. (Ephesians 2:10, Amplified Bible)

I would rehearse this notion over and over in my thoughts—God prepared beforehand the things that I would do. He saw me doing great things for *Him*.

Once I began to understand how God loves—that His love isn't based on my "performance"—I became more relaxed. He was offering me unconditional love, and all I had to do was to simply receive it. I grew in my understanding of who I was and who I belonged to—that I was a child of the creator.

I opened up to the idea that I had purposes and that God had designed me to walk them out. I was called to live a life of victory, and I began to step out into new things.

CHAPTER 9

The Past Resurfaces

Even though I had victory in most areas of my life, I was still pretending to be what I thought everyone wanted me to be. Of course I didn't realize it at the time.

Life led me to landing a job as an office manager/DC assistant for a new chiropractic office. Though the position was intimidating to me, everyone believed that I could do it. And not wanting to disappoint anyone, I took the position—even though I had huge doubts that I was the gal for the job. Things got overwhelming, but I thought I had everything under control. Every day, I reminded myself that God would equip me with all that I needed (2 Timothy 3:17).

But one June day, everything quickly spun out of control. I received an unsettling phone call while I was at a conference in Chicago for work. I wasn't told specifics, only that I was needed several states away—that I had a family member in the hospital.

I cannot explain the severe fear that seized me. It truly was as if someone had a tight grip on my throat and I was gasping for air. All the worst-case scenarios ran through my mind. I knew that this was a new kind of battle—something I hadn't encountered before. Intense terror was washing over me like a giant ocean wave, and it was crippling me. The hours between the call and finding out what was going on were the longest and hardest hours I'd had to endure up to that point in my life. I had to consciously keep my focus on the Lord. I seriously had to imagine heaven encamped around my loved one. I used my mind's eye like never before. I would see God's glory invade the darkness that I believed was trying to gather around me and my family.

Then I heard it. I've heard it before—a small, little voice inside me. And it said, "Just as you have gone through things, you will be able to help others." What was startling for me in that moment was that I identified instantly what the words meant. I hadn't thought about what had happened to me when I was a young girl, not since I had accepted Jesus as my personal savior. I mean, the old was gone, and I was new, right?

I felt I was being crushed under a huge weight! I never wanted this type of thing to happen to anyone I knew, especially someone in my own family. Instantly I became determined that I would be in this person's corner. I wasn't going to let years of destructive self-image and extreme darkness take control over my loved one's life like they had mine.

No! I became determined. Deep inside myself, I drew a line in the sand—the enemy of our souls would not have my family.

I wasn't about to stand by and allow years of self-hatred and a cold, colorless life affect her like it had me. *No.*

♥ ♥ ♥

Weeks had passed since that call. I'd tried to get her to meet with me so that we could talk after I got out of work, but it never happened. I knew what she was doing. She was filling every minute with noise so that she didn't have to be alone with her thoughts. I had been there; I think we all have. It's just easier to deal with life than it is to sort out whether the voice inside is speaking truth or telling a destructive lie.

I felt that I needed to help her process what had happened to her. In my heart, I believed that if she got healing right away, she wouldn't find herself years later in the position I had been in—wondering who she was.

I knew who I was. I was a child of God, a new creation. I was free, or at least that is what I thought I was. With this belief that I had been freed and that I possessed such wisdom, I would ask God often throughout my day, How I can help her through this?

As desperate as I was to hear an answer, I never got one.

At work, my thoughts on how to support and get healing for my family consumed me. I realized that I couldn't deal with the demands at work and my own raw emotions that I felt about this family member's assault. I knew I couldn't give 100 percent to all my responsibilities. That was when I told the doctor I worked for that he would have to find my replacement.

Eight weeks after our conversation, I resigned. I was home, making myself available to talk with and console anyone who needed help processing what had unfolded in our lives.

Even though I was home all day, no one stopped by to talk. Slowly, each day became unnervingly silent for me. All the busyness I experienced up to that point had a rhythm and pace about it. But once the noise of work was no longer there, I didn't know what to do with myself.

The noise of my life was easier to deal with than the questions that rose up within me. Each time I had asked God how I could help my family, I wouldn't hear that still, small voice that I had heard before.

I know this sounds somewhat odd, but I wasn't consciously looking at my own past. I knew there was a darkness that I had gotten over, but I didn't define it to myself.

Does that even make sense? I really don't know how to explain this. I knew that something had happened to me—that I had been taken advantage of. But it was just words. No mental picture was tied to the words. Think of it this way. If you say the word *horse*, it doesn't really impact you unless you mentally see a tall, strong horse with a black, shiny coat running into the wind, its long mane bouncing with each galloping step. See what I mean?

I identified that I had struggled with a lack of self-worth and fought for years to even like myself. But that was as far as I could acknowledge my past. I had no clue that I was walking in denial.

Yet each time I asked a question, another would rise within me that would make me feel more uncomfortable. I was confronting questions such as, Are you sure you have healing from your past? It got to the point that I truly felt those doubting questions were coming from the accuser.

Frightened to explore what was stirring inside me, I would push it aside saying, "I am a child of God and the past is gone. I am a new creation in Christ Jesus" (2 Corinthians 5:17).

One clear morning

Then one morning as the sun was peaking over the horizon, I stepped out the back door, as I had often done to go for my morning walk. The air wasn't heavy with humidity. I felt as if I could breathe easier, and my mind felt fresh.

Hearing the gravel roll under each step, I got lost in my thoughts once more. Once again, I was pondering the same questions I had been pondering for weeks. I asked God, "How can I help my family? All of them seem to be walking in denial, doing life as usual. How did I work through my own darkness?"

Then suddenly, I heard that small voice! It totally took me off guard, especially what the voice said to me—"You didn't."

What?! This answer seemed to have come from nowhere. It

had never crossed my mind that I hadn't been healed from my past. I once more blamed the accuser for the things that I was hearing.

Of course the accuser would like me to believe I didn't have healing, I told myself. *He is just trying to make me feel pain from my past. But I know who I am. I am a new creation in Christ.*

Then I could almost hear God chuckle at me. "Are you seriously going to quote scripture to Me, Georgia? I know that you are a new creation, and I am telling you, My daughter, you have never processed what happened to you."

That's when my mind was flooded with even more questions:

What did that mean?

Did these questions come from within me?

Was I supposed to seek answers to them?

What was I supposed to do?

It was as if I had fallen into a rushing river that I couldn't tame. Emotionally, I struggled to keep myself from being fully immersed under water, my world spinning. I walked quickly back home as I fought to make sense of what I had heard. I had no clue what I was supposed to do. Or maybe I was afraid of what I was supposed to do. Still in denial, I ended up reasoning that the real question wasn't about my healing. Mentally, I once again shut the door on that subject, though it was getting harder to do.

The wall

Trying to hush the thoughts stirring inside me, I became demanding with my family. "We need to 'talk' so we can 'work through' what happened," I would shout. "You need to go to counseling and not to bottle things up inside," I would say. "Remember you are a child of God and anything negative you might hear in your head comes from the enemy of your soul."

I wasn't hearing my own words, as I believed that I had been set free. But subconsciously, I was trying to tell myself these things.

Don't get me wrong. I had found freedom in many areas of my life. But there was an area that wasn't open for discussion—not even with God. And to be truthful, at the time, I didn't even realize my past was an issue. Up to that point of my life, I had made up who I was. What I mean is that I had cut all the bad stuff out of my life and remodeled myself to the person I showed the world. "I am a new creation."

Peaking over my shoulder

As I was now alone every day without the noise of a set schedule, my world became very silent. I didn't have to be at work on time. I didn't have daunting tasks at home. And my youngest didn't really need me, being that he was a junior in high school.

I had no one to place demands on me or my time. This only allowed those haunting questions to become louder. The questions were requiring me to be honest with myself. I couldn't dance around the issue anymore. Sweeping it under the rug wasn't going to work, and the closet door wouldn't even open to stuff in there. Nope, my past was rising up as sure as the sun rises.

Looking back on my life since high school, I can see that I have always kept myself busy, living a noisy life. I worked several jobs at the same time. And once I was married, I would get involved in huge projects that kept me exhausted. I didn't have time to allow the little girl inside ask the adult woman those stupid questions; they weren't important. And I didn't feel as if I had to acknowledge them.

But now that my world was quiet, the questions got louder. Things in my life began to move in slow motion, and as I acknowledged that I could hear my younger self, my world stopped. I stopped running on the treadmill (so to speak) that

Georgia Barnes

I had been on. I wasn't even walking a fast pace. Everything stopped, and that was when I slowly glanced over my shoulder to look at my past.

We all do this. We align ourselves with the rhythm and pace around us. One day leads to another, and then another goes by. Before we know it, we have stuffed the hurts so deep that we don't even know those things affect us.

But as the noises of our lives become silent, that's when it happens. We hear it—the still, small voice. And it is calling us to something uncharted, foreign, and even uncomfortable. *What is this? Where is it coming from?* we ask ourselves.

The only one who knew about my past was my husband, Bob. No one knew that I'd had a child before I had gotten married— not our friends or even the members of the church we belonged to. My mentors who I'd had over the years didn't know about the dark destructive dreams that haunted me when I closed my eyes at night.

Up to that point, I had tried to piece together only a few things about my childhood to make up for the years. I purposely threw out all that was dark and ugly to me, convincing myself that those parts of my life and past did not exist.

If ever my past would try to surface, I would tell myself I was a new creation as I pushed those memories back down again.

Nevertheless, all of the things that I had learned about who I am and who I belonged to weren't working for me this time. I started to become intimidated and insecure like I had been before, afraid of what people would think of me if they knew I had given up my baby. Even though I knew I had been accepted, I had a huge fear that my past would disqualify me.

Verbalize out loud

One day, out of the blue, I asked my mother, "What was the name given on 'her' birth certificate?" I was surprised I had articulated the question out loud. It was only a whisper I had asked myself a few days earlier.

The odd thing about it, though, was that my mom knew what I meant. She didn't ask me why I was asking. She just gave me the information and left the subject alone.

Subconsciously, I did too; I left the subject alone.

Maybe if I stopped poking at it (my past) it would stop trying to breathe (come alive).

I tried hard to focus on other things. However, I kept running into this uncommon name my mom had told me.

It was the very name of the winner of a game show my husband was watching. I was in the kitchen cooking dinner when the host of the show was loudly announcing that T—— had just won; I about jumped out of my pants.

I went to the local pharmacy to get my husband's medicine, and the gal behind the counter had a name tag on. I looked at her name tag so I could address her. I about choked to pronounce "it" out loud. Again, *that* name was there in front of me. I instantly felt shame when I said her name—as if everyone in earshot knew what that name meant to me. Shame washed over me. It was as if I was fifteen and pregnant again, and I was getting all those disappointing looks that had been a part of my everyday life back then.

I wanted to run out of the pharmacy to escape the uncomfortable feeling I had. But how does one run away from something within?

Getting on with my life

Days later, I finally threw my hand up to the Lord and said, "Okay, Lord, I am going to stop trying to figure this out. Obviously, I am not supposed to make myself available to my family to talk. I just pray Your peace and love will cover over us all. Now let me just get on with my life. No more looking at my past—let me get on with today."

Later that afternoon I found myself at our local home improvement store. Even though I had no reason to be there, I randomly walked the aisle. After seeing the colorful display of flowers outside, I decided to buy some plants. The mums looked beautiful, and I picked out the colors I liked.

When I placed them in my cart, I noticed the tags of the other flowers on display. *That's strange*, I said to myself. *These flowers have real names.* Out of curiosity, I looked over to read the name of the mums that I had placed in my cart. As I did, my mind went spinning. I tried to mentally grasp what I had just read. I couldn't believe it. There her name was again—Tabitha!

I wanted to get out of the store as soon as I could. I was the only one in the garden area, so I rushed to the cashier to pay for my flowers. That was when the cashier pointed out to me that the mums had *real* names. She didn't just note it once, but instead she pointed it out three times, each time becoming more enthusiastic. The conversation went like this:

"What pretty flowers you picked out today. Did you notice that they have *real* names?" she asked.

"Yes I did," I responded.

"Yeah, and did you see that huge beautiful flowerpot of mums sitting in front of the display? Aren't they beautiful? And the flowers have *real* names."

"Yes! That is a beautiful plant."

"The names are beautiful too! Those are *real* names, you know."

By then, my heart was pounding. I got so nervous I was shaking. I paid for the flowers and rushed to my car. Once inside, I had to just sit there for a moment. My heart was pounding hard and my head was spinning. *What just happened?* I asked myself. I don't even recall driving back home.

Questions came rushing into my mind.

"Yes, I noticed the names, God!"

"Are You trying to tell me something?"

"Are You trying to get my attention?"

"What is it that You want me to do?"

"Do You want me to look for this person?"

"I am not sure I want to do that."

"What does she think of me?"

"Would she be ashamed of me or maybe angry with me?"

"No, Lord, her life is better off without me. I don't want to do this!"

As these questions whirled around in my head and I thought about what had just happened, my anxieties grew.

Would I have to meet this person? I thought to myself. I just wanted to put everything about my past back where it was before it got disrupted.

My past was becoming more and more real to me. It was up in my face and I didn't know how to deal with it. I must have buried deep in my subconscious all the memories of, and emotions, associated with what had happened to me that summer long ago. And honestly that was where I wanted them to return. I told myself I wasn't about to let the enemy put shame on me again and tell me lies about who I am. I told myself to stand on the truth of what God said about me and to remember that I was a *new creation*.

As I mentally told myself all these things, these words rose up within me: "It is not always about *you*. She is looking for you, and you need to prepare yourself and your family. There have been times that she has been close to finding you, but I have closed the door because *you* were not ready. Your paths *will* cross. You need to prepare yourself."

Then I saw a image of a puzzle completed except for one piece. I was holding the missing piece in my hand, afraid to put it in its place.

These words and this vision were so real to me. I was scared. By then, I was on my knees out in the backyard crying uncontrollably.

"Was that You, Lord God? What do You mean that she has been close to finding me? Was she really looking for me? I am sure that her life has been complete with her adoptive family. Why would someone want to look for me? This is crazy!"

Then it finally dawned on me! Could it be that I really hadn't dealt with my past? Really, how could I tell my loved one not to run from their hurt and let God heal and restore them if I haven't done it myself?

The rest of the afternoon and evening, I did what I normally do; I busied myself, trying to brush away all that had happened earlier that day.

I am reading too much into this, I told myself.

I had convinced myself that what had happened earlier in the day was just my imagination getting away from me. But still, I couldn't help feeling afraid—that someone would find me.

Flipping through the television stations

I was alone at home again. So I randomly searched for something on TV to occupy my thoughts. I paused briefly on a show and found myself drawn in. The scenario struck such deep emotions within me—so much that I felt as if I was in the twilight zone.

The story was about a young girl who got sent away when she found herself pregnant to a school for unwed, young mothers. Shame washed over me because there was something familiar about what I was watching. As the story unfolded, I felt like I was reeling a fishing line up from a deep, deep place I didn't even know was there. I could sense that there was something big on the other end. And it scared me. As I struggled to see what was pulling so hard on the other end of the fishing line, bits and pieces of my past was surfacing.

Always before, when bad memories would surface, I could push them back down. I would tell myself that it was just a bad dream—that it hadn't really happened to me. But now, this time, watching (in some way) my life on the television screen was too much.

I couldn't believe that I was being tormented like this.

"Okay, Lord! What are You asking me to do? Am I to look for this person? Or am I supposed to pray for her? *What* is it that You want me to do?"

CHAPTER 10

Doing Something!

I did it! I called the county clerk's office of the county where I had given birth and asked the clerk a "hypothetical" question.

The phone rang once, and right away, a woman answered.

Shocked that someone answered, I responded clumsily, unprepared to talk. "If someone had placed their baby up for adoption and the files were closed, how would one go about opening them back up?" I began. "This friend of mine knows the name given on the birth certificate."

The clerk then told me that when a child was put up for adoption, "The original birth certificate is destroyed."

My heart instantly broke, and a sadness that I had never experienced before washed over me. It was like my biggest fear was true: *I really didn't matter.* I had been erased completely from my daughter's life.

As I tried to keep from crying, the clerk went on to say other things to me, but I couldn't hear her. I was too overwhelmed with grief.

However, I finally did hear her gently address me. "I am thankful you went through with the pregnancy," she told me. "What you did was brave and a selfless thing to do at such a young age. So many other girls would have taken a different approach under the circumstances."

Then she went on to say, "If you are wanting to open the files, all I need from you is a form signed by you and a witness. Would you like me to send that to you?"

I didn't know when the conversation went from a hypothetical question to the clerk addressing me personally as the birth mother. But I ended up giving her my address and said goodbye. I didn't know why I had given her my address; I knew I wasn't really going to do anything with the form she'd said she would send.

After getting off the phone with the clerk, I cried. This was like no cry I had ever had before. It was a deep sob, and at the time, I couldn't understand why I felt so broken. I guess I was experiencing feelings I had bottled up for years. Unidentified emotions were coming out of me, and I had no clue why.

I had always told myself that I was in a good place, and I was happy. I mean, I was a child of God. Why would I not be happy, right?

Realizing all that had unfolded over the months, I told myself again, *This really isn't about you. It is about your loved one and family members getting their healing.*

All of a sudden, I immediately stopped crying and pulled myself together, gaining control of my emotions. I pushed everything back down. It was as if I was swallowing a huge pill.

I went into my bathroom and cleaned up my face and went about cleaning the house. I wasn't going to allow myself to look over my shoulder any more. That was enough looking back at my past. I had my cry. I could now move on.

I am a grown woman and have a family and responsibilities, I thought to myself. I couldn't spend time going back to when I was a little girl. This was now, and the Bible did say, "Forget the former things; do not dwell in the past" (Isaiah 43:18).

After my emotional breakdown, I pushed myself even harder to get things done around the house. I started all sorts of projects but didn't finish them. I was going in every direction but not getting anywhere. I did my best to keep myself busy.

My days were so full that it seemed like weeks had gone by since I'd made that phone call to the county clerk. Sometime that following week, I was instantly pulled back to that conversation when I went to the mailbox and pulled out one single envelope with a return address that read "County Courthouse."

Oh my goodness! I felt everyone on my street knew what I had just received in the mailbox. I quickly went inside the house and stuffed the envelope into back of my Bible case.

Again, trying to push this all out of my thoughts, I struggled to set my mind to the here and now. I had to stop allowing my thoughts to pull me back in time.

A Deep Dream

Have you ever awakened from such a deep sleep that it takes you a moment to figure out where you are and how long you've been sleeping?

What seemed like days was only hours after my husband left for work. The light instantly blinded me as my lids began to open. With a sense of being lost, I tried to pull myself to consciousness. It felt as if sand bags were tied to my legs as I fought to swing them to the edge of the bed.

Struggling to shake myself awake, I found myself asking, "What day is it? Where is everybody?"

In a mental fog, I stumbled to the kitchen to make myself a pot of joe. Systematically, I opened the coffee and tossed two scoops into the coffee maker, and while filling the water basin, the dream I had the night before became vividly clear. It was so real that it frightened me, and I dropped the coffeepot into the sink. Again, I asked myself, *What does this all mean?*

My dream

In this dream there were two of Me's. One was standing between two rooms, but they were at two totally different places. To my left was a high-end restaurant. It was a room with soft, glowing lights, and everyone was enjoying his or her meal. The other room, to my right, was a brightly lit school classroom. In the classroom, there were people sitting with their babies on their laps and a piece of paper on top of the desks. The instructor in the classroom told all of us to write out why we needed to place our babies up for adoption. I was one of those sitting at a desk. However, instead of a baby girl on my lap, I had a baby boy.

I kept looking up at everybody in the room busy writing. Then I would look back down at my own paper, lost for words. I looked over and could see the room to my left side, the restaurant. The cashier was my loved one who had been assaulted, and she was struggling to get everyone checked out.

It was like I could hear the thoughts of the me that was in the classroom: *I will fill out this paper in a minute. I just want to go over there and help her. Once I am done helping get everyone checked out, I will come back and fill out the paperwork.*

I watched myself walk over to the restaurant and jump right in to help. Together we cashed out the many people waiting to pay their bill. We then balanced the register and finished cleaning up after the event.

All of a sudden I looked over at the classroom. Again, I could hear my thoughts: *Oh my goodness. Everyone is gone!*

I ran back to the classroom, which was still brightly lit, and stood looking at all the empty desks. Then my eyes stopped at the desk I had been sitting at. The only evidence that anyone was there before was the very piece of paper I needed to fill out. My baby was even gone, and I quietly began to cry. I felt so completely empty.

♥♥♥

As I thought about the dream, I stood up and declared, "This dream has nothing to do with what was going on in my life."

I then pushed the images of that dream to the same place I pushed all my surfacing emotions, somewhere deep inside, and secured them there with a lock. Subconsciously, I threw away the key.

But as I kept running into the name *Tabitha*, I resolved that maybe the Lord wanted me to pray for her.

I could do that; I only wanted good for Tabitha. So I prayed that she had a good man in her life, that she was treated well, and that she had a godly mother who would give her wisdom when she needed it. And I left it at that.

But still, every time I tried to move forward and wash my hands of all of this (my past) the Lord wouldn't let me. I tried to focus on my husband and family, working in the yard, cleaning the house. I did anything to get my thoughts off of my past, but my efforts to ignore it weren't working.

It was like each time I walked around the obstacle of the past I was trying to avoid, God would pick it back up and put it back in my path. I couldn't shake my past, and I felt fear and shame paralyze me.

I saw myself on the edge of a very dark forest, with dark, thick muck all around, and I was being made to walk through it. No one knew that the forest existed or that I was facing it. I felt alone and scared. Peering into the darkness, I couldn't make out exactly what I was about to step into, let alone what sorts of things I would encounter. I was almost certain I would get hurt.

And every time I tried to turn away and go another direction, I found myself in front of the same dark forest.

Anxiety was getting the best of me. Fear that I would be judged by other people made me lose my breath.

What would people say about me?

Would my Christian friends say I was a bad mom, like I had been told in high school?

With those thoughts, I told the Lord again, "I don't want to look at this. I am okay with my past buried."

A few days later, I was reading scripture, and I felt the Lord was trying to comfort and encourage me to move forward. In Isaiah 54:4, I read, "Do not be afraid; you will not suffer shame. Do not fear disgrace; you will not be humiliated. You will forget the shame of your youth."

My past was spouting up within me with such great force that I could no longer ignore it. It would be like trying to cap off a gushing geyser; it was impossible. That was how it was with my past; it just wouldn't stop surfacing.

I truly believed that who I was back then didn't matter—that the experiences I had gone through as a kid didn't make the adult person I was now. I guess, in some ways, I separated the younger me from the adult me. I didn't even realize that who I was and how I interacted (or reacted) had a lot of to do with what I had experienced as a young person.

Still uncertain what all of these things meant, I agreed with the nudging that I had been getting in my spirit to go ahead and fill out the papers—to open the files.

One Simple Signature

I sat staring at the form I had received in the mail—the form that would start the process of opening the adoption files. All I had to do was one simple act—sign my name. I had done it many times over the years, but this one signature would impact my world.

Would it be okay?

Would I be judged?

Would it confirm that I was a bad mom?

I was totally releasing control of this whole situation by signing my name on this simple form. I was opening myself to uncertainty and vulnerability—to my future, but what type of future?

As I held the ink pen in my hand, I thought of how I wished I could have been more—done more in my life to be type of person others could be proud of. But I was just me.

Even though I felt uncertain of what my future held, I was more convinced than ever that the Lord was nudging me to do this.

All the signs leading up to this point were too much to deny. But I still felt as if I was jumping off a cliff.

By signing this form, I had to admit that it had all been real and not a dream. Years of denial would instantly appear within the tapestry of my life - a past I hardly acknowledged.

Really, though, it had always been there. I had just refused to see it. Then suddenly, there it was—as if it had magically appeared the moment I threw the stamped envelope that held the signed request to open the adoption files in the mail.

I was on autopilot as I walked the envelope containing this form to the mailbox. Trying to pretend the impact this would make on my life was no big deal, I told myself, *It's not like this person will be at my doorstep tomorrow.*

I did it. It was done—over. I had done what I felt the Lord was leading me to do. *Now,* I thought to myself, *I can move on.*

CHAPTER 11

Moving Forward

I would like to say that, instantly, the lines of communication between me and the person in my family who had been attacked were opened. But they weren't. I decided it was time for me to move forward and get on with my life. Given that I'd resigned from the position I had held when I was at the conference in Chicago, I updated my résumé and started applying for different jobs.

I hadn't gotten too far along in my search, however, when my mother-in-law, Aileen, was in a bad car accident. I wasn't working, so I was available to be with her most everyday while she was in the hospital. Being there with her distracted me from myself. I could busy myself with taking care of her, instead of trying to figure out how to process my past. And that was a relief for me.

My world began to get loud again, filled with daily reports from health care providers and need for organization and planning. I was, once again, busy. I wanted to make sure my mother-in-law was being taken care of and to advocate for her if I felt that wasn't the case.

My thoughts never wandered back to what had weighed on me before the accident. I was driven to be at the hospital most every day. Quickly (miraculously) my mother-in-law improved, and after being in the hospital for approximately a month, she was released to home care.

My husband and I talked it over with other family members and decided to have her live with us (until she could be on her own again). Having her stay with us was a bit more demanding than I had anticipated, with all the different doctor visits. But again, I was thankful for the distraction.

The Phone Rings

One evening in November, a phone call came in—heralding in a night that I will never forget for the rest of my life. We were settling in, trying to decide what to watch on television, when the phone rang.

I figured whoever was calling must be looking for Kory, my son. So I let him answer it. But he shrugged his shoulders as he handed the phone to me.

I said, "Hello?"

The person on the other end said, "Hello, is this Georgia?"

"Yes," I said.

The next words this person said to me made my heart jump into my mouth! Through sobs she said, "Hi! My name is Lisa, and I am your daughter."

Oh my God! I gasped. Instantly, I felt fear grip me. I couldn't believe what I had just heard! Had I heard this person right? Was I dreaming? Oh my word, this is it! This is the person I had been afraid to meet for twenty-six years? She had found me!

I felt that I kept my voice calm as I spoke, but I was so afraid. I am just thankful it was a phone call and not a knock at my front door. Don't get me wrong; I was happy she had reached out to me, but the shame I'd felt when I was a high school girl surfaced instantly.

So many thoughts were going through my head. All the while I was trying to have the most important conversation of my life. It was all too much to maneuver through. I was trying to sound like a woman who had it all together, but I felt like I was having an out-of-body experience.

How does one have a conversation with God as they talk to a person on the phone? I don't know, but that was what I did. I asked God what I was supposed to do.

What was the right way to feel?

What was the right thing to say?

Does she hate me for placing her up for adoption?

Was she going to see me as the unaccomplished woman that I felt I was?

Would she be embarrassed of me and wish she'd never contacted me?

I was so afraid. And even though I was conversing with her, the impact of what was occurring just wasn't sinking in. It was too big to understand. So many things whirled in my head. And to be completely honest, I think I was in shock. My mouth was on autopilot as I answered her questions and asked general ones back. I wanted her to feel comfortable, but I didn't know if I felt comfortable.

She sounded so sweet. Was it really her?

I felt compelled to tell her why she was placed in adoption. I don't even know if she asked me why. With all my guilt and shame, I thought that must be the only reason she had called me.

Lisa told me about her fiancé, Kevin, and how he was good to her. She also told me that she had always wanted to know her biological mother, but something always kept her from seeking. It was Kevin who had encouraged her to fill out the appropriate paperwork to get information from the court.

When she told me when she'd finally requested information

about me, I instantly had goose bumps and let out a gasp. It was only five days after I had signed and mailed the release form to open the files.

We talked and cried for about thirty minutes. And as we were ending our conversation, I gave her my email address and asked her to email me. I thought through email we could possibly start a relationship, whatever kind of relationship it would be.

Telling the kids about Lisa

I had shared with Bob about my past before we decided to get married. And little did I know, he secretly prayed that my daughter and I would one day be reunited. However, it was never talked about around the kids.

Each time Lisa and I would talk, she would ask me if I had told Ashley and Kory about her. She was so excited to learn about her sister and brother and was looking forward to building a relationship with them.

I felt uncomfortable telling her that I hadn't yet. I was enjoying it being just her and me. Perhaps I was being selfish, but I liked it that way. I liked that we were getting to know each other without me having to share her with anyone else or worrying about how the news would be received. Besides, I had no clue how to approach Ashley and Kory with this. It wasn't long after the first few conversations that I could hear disappointment in her voice each time she asked if I had told them about her.

The longer I held on to my secret, the more fear I felt about how they would react. Even though I started to feel guilty for keep Lisa to myself, the fear was stronger, and it kept me paralyzed.

It was then I heard an inner voice (not audible, but something within) tell me, *It isn't always about you.*

I then realized that by not telling Ashley and Kory about Lisa, I was hurting Lisa. This voice went on to say that I wasn't showing unconditional love to Lisa. I was more concerned about how uncomfortable I was going to feel. Wondering how Ashley and Kory would think of me scared me the most. Would they tell me that I was the "worst mom ever" once they found out that I had had a child before they were born? I wouldn't be able to handle it if my children rejected me, their mom, because of my past.

Nevertheless, I did come up with a plan. My goal was to get Ashley and Kory together and tell them that they had a sister who very much wanted to meet them. I secretly wished there were some sort of guide to read—dos and don'ts of telling your children that they have a sibling they never knew about. I had many questions for the Lord on how to approach this subject, but I never heard any answers.

This was such an overwhelming task for me. Yes, I had spent many times on the phone with Lisa, and we'd exchanged countless emails. But still, it wasn't really registering inside my head that she *is* my daughter!

Sharing Lisa with Ashley and Kory would make it real to me—*who* she really was, my daughter. Even though I had gotten past opening the adoption files and had had conversations with Lisa, I was dealing with only little pieces of my past, not the whole picture. I was still functioning in denial.

Imagine a small girl hiding behind a huge tree, and she senses that there is something big on the other side—something *big* in stature, bigger than her. Nervously, she peeks around to get a quick look at it. But she doesn't look long enough to even make out what she was seeing, as she is too frightened.

This is how I felt. I knew this would be something huge in my life. But I was still too afraid to look long enough to figure it out. A peek here and there was enough. I couldn't stare at it, as that would mean I had to react.

My prayer was that we all could accept each other and could

blend together, each building the different relationships within the larger circle.

I think I was most afraid of how Ashley would feel when she learned she wasn't the only daughter. Would she feel less valued? Would she hate me for giving her sister away? Would she understand why I had done what I did?

I would often play out in my head how the conversation would go. I even imagined what my children's responses would be. It was like I was setting up dominos (so to speak). If the conversation went as I rehearsed, everything would be good. This type of mapping drove me close to a nervous breakdown—a repetitious pattern I have habitually done in many areas of my life.

Each day that I planned to get them together, the plan would fail, and then another day would pass. I couldn't get them both to stay home long enough to talk with them.

My mother-in-law living with us made my planned moment even harder to achieve. We tried to keep family matters to ourselves so that we wouldn't make her feel even more uneasy about staying at our house than she already was. Coincidentally, and again miraculously, Aileen was able to return home after being with us for a little over two months.

I ended up telling Ashley first. We were in the kitchen, and I just opened the conversation by telling her that I had something difficult to share. Right away, she asked if I was pregnant.

"No, I am not pregnant," I said.

"You found your other daughter?" she asked.

I was shocked that she guessed it and even more surprised that she remembered what I had tried to tell her about my first child when she was in high school.

Was this something that she had secretly hoped for? Did she have thoughts about what had happened to me and never asked?

Did her knowing that I had given my rights up as a mother before make her feel insecure in our relationship?

Nope. There was no more beating around the bush. I couldn't retreat and hide. I had to push through and answer her questions.

"No, she found me," I told her.

Ashley acted surprised and excited, though something inside me made me think she had some idea that Lisa and I had found each other.

As I tried to tell Ashley how the whole thing had unfolded and how much of a struggle it was for me to find the words to tell her and Kory, she seemed preoccupied with her own thoughts.

As soon as Ashley heard I had pictures of Lisa, she asked to see them. I was on autopilot from there on. My thoughts were whirling around in my head as I went to the computer and pulled up her photo.

This is it! I thought. And I prayed that it would turn out all right.

I couldn't read Ashley's reaction when she was staring at the pictures. She seemed excited, but I wasn't sure. It was as if she was holding her breath. And once she did finally exhale, she said, "Mom, she really looks like you."

I wasn't as nervous telling Kory about Lisa as I had been with Ashley. I explained that I was in a bad situation in which I had become pregnant, and because of the circumstances, I had placed my baby for adoption. It had been twenty-six years, and she had found me. "She really would like to meet us," I told him.

Kory's first response was anger. It seemed he wasn't as naive as I would have hoped; he wanted to know the details of the "bad situation." In a way, he is similar to my husband. Bob also wanted to seek justice!

As much as he wanted me to answer those questions, I told

him that out of a negative situation we now had something miraculous enter our lives. We had Lisa.

As I showed him the picture of her, he wore the same expression I had seen on Ashley's face. "She really looks like you, Mom," he said.

I then proceeded to introduce them all via email. I didn't read what Ashley or Kory said to Lisa. However, I hoped they would have email dialogue with each other before the pending face-to-face reunion.

CHAPTER 12

So When Should We Meet?

I really wanted to meet Lisa, though I wasn't sure what I needed to do to prepare for the reunion. I knew she would have a lot of questions, but I wasn't sure I could answer them. I had stuffed my past so deep that I didn't even know if I could find the emotions, thoughts, and fears that I'd had back then. We finally set the date for February 22, 2008.

I never got to hold Lisa after I gave birth to her. I didn't even get to see her, not a glimpse of her hair or her little hand. She was quickly removed from me by the health care professionals.

It just overwhelmed me to think that I was going to meet this young woman who was my daughter for the first time. I didn't even begin to know how to comprehend this; I couldn't turn and run away. It was like I was being led one step at a time to something big. This was really going to happen.

From day one, Ashley and Kory grew up knowing me. They would stare at my face as I fed, bathed, and clothed them. When they were babies, they would search my eyes when they were upset to find comfort.

And over the years, they had grown to read my facial expressions. They knew when I tried to stuff my tears, and they knew when I was trying to be fearless when I was afraid. I am sure that they could sense the emotional roller coaster I was on. I only can assume they were on one as well, but they never said anything. Not even my husband Bob talked with me about how I was dealing with everything.

Truthfully, though, asking me how to prepare for what was about to happen wouldn't have done them any good again—I couldn't get my head around it myself. The Lord must have given Ashley and Kory wisdom because they never once asked me questions as I tried to work through the chaos going on in my head and heart. They all gave me my space; it was like they weren't even around. Or maybe they were, and I was so consumed with my own dialogue that I didn't acknowledge anyone else.

Processing

Everyone knows that there is a natural bond between mother and child that grows from the first day we mothers hold our babies in our arms. But this was different. Yes, Lisa was my daughter. However she didn't know me. Would she accept me? Would she even like me?

In preparation for our meeting, I thought I had to remember what I had spent twenty-six years forgetting. But even still, I couldn't fully go back to that time of my life. I couldn't find the courage to make myself remember the things I'd spent too long trying to forget.

Meeting Lisa

Lisa and I grew more comfortable with each other through our emails, and we started talking more on the telephone. She shared more things about her childhood and talked about her fiancé, Kevin. They had been engaged for a while, as they were saving the money to pay for their wedding on their own. She also told me that she couldn't decide on a wedding date.

I personally believed that because Lisa didn't understand unconditional love, she had a hard time understanding Kevin's love. Even more reason, I thought, for me to work though my past before we met. I didn't want her to mistake my own self-rejection as a rejection of her.

To my surprise, in one of our phone conversations, Lisa announced that she and Kevin had picked a wedding date. She wanted to get married on May 11, 2008, Mother's Day, and she asked me if I could be there.

I couldn't believe it! My long-lost daughter was planning one of the most memorable events in her life, and she wanted us there! It would be a day spent making memories that would be forever engraved in their hearts and they (she) wanted us (me) there.

After we got off the phone, I just sat quietly and cried. My head whirled again. This was unbelievable! Lisa wanted me to be at her wedding. Then oh-my-gosh thoughts ran through my head: Her family and friends will be there. What will they think of me? Will Ashley and Kory be okay with this?

The final push

With our reunion date quickly approaching I knew I needed to stop with all my busyness. I needed to stop worrying about my family or the diet that I thought I should start or deep cleaning the house. I had to force myself to stop the crazy demands I placed on myself so that I could finally meet the person that I had been running from—me.

In all honestly, I had thought up to that point in my life that I knew me. But I didn't. I knew the pretend me, the made-up person I was choosing to be. By picking and choosing only parts of my past, I wasn't being honest with the most important person—myself. I had custom-designed my life; some things were allowed in my memory, and some things were just cut out. Seriously, up until that point, I hadn't even known I was doing that. I had no clue how paralyzing my suppressed past was—that it was keeping me from fully moving forward in my life. I then became fully aware that for all these years I had been stuck.

Yes, I always felt I was hiding from something. It was like a shadow—sometimes I would see it, and sometimes I wouldn't. I never felt too comfortable. I was always wondering when the other shoe would drop. Even after I accepted Jesus as my savior, I thought it would only be a matter of time before my life would fall apart. I never realized that behind all this fear there was one thing I feared the most—and that was actually me.

How does one stop and evaluate his or her life completely— the good, the bad, and the ugly? I pondered this question. I knew that I didn't want to experience the vulnerability I had felt when I was younger. But I couldn't go back where I had been all these years— in denial. What I mean to say is that I got a glimpse of myself, and I couldn't deny *her* anymore.

I realized that over the years I had let God have different areas of my heart, but never had I given Him my whole heart.

Let me describe it like this: Take a piece of clay and roll it in a ball. Put a big hole in the center and then close the bottom of the ball. The clay ball looks round and solid, but there is still a hole in the center. Now take this clay ball and make marks on it, scratches and divots from being bumped around. Each day, cover the ball with another layer of clay and put more scratches and divots on it. Now repeat this last step year after year. What is happening to the hole? It is getting deeper and deeper in the center. That was my heart. Over the years, I showed God those scratches and divots. And yes, He has healed the marks engraved on each layer of my heart. But this hole in my heart was so deep I didn't even know it was there. God knew about the hole, though, and He waited patiently for me to trust Him enough to show Him my deepest wound of all.

I finally came out of hiding, and in doing so, I found the little girl crying in the corner of my life. God knew she was there, but I didn't. That is when I could see in my mind's eye God picking up this little girl (me) from the corner and sitting her on His lap. And as I shared everything I could about that memory, what had happened, and what I had come to believe about myself, He listened. I felt a peace and love wash over me that I had never experienced. Then, as a gentle whisper within me I heard Him say, "I never said those things about you that you believe about yourself. You need to understand that My love and grace covers you from head to toe. It covers your past, present, and even your future. It is all covered. I am removing your sadness and restoring you. You are My daughter, and I love you."

The reunion

I had walked through the dark forest that I felt nudged to walk though. I had allowed memories to fully surface, not forcing them up but neither forcing them down. I just allowed myself to remember. It was all now real to me; it wasn't just a dream or a story that I vaguely remembered. It all really happened to me, and it was a part of who I am.

I felt that this was as close as I was going to get to being ready to meet Lisa. Yet again, I had to ask myself, *How does a person prepare to meet a grown woman who once grew inside of her?* It wasn't like I was just meeting a random young couple for dinner. This was my daughter and her fiancé!

We agreed to meet on neutral ground, so to speak, neither at her place nor mine. We would meet halfway. We made weekend reservations at the same hotel at the halfway mark between the two homes. The plan was that I would first meet Lisa alone in her hotel room, and then after an hour or so, I would introduce her to Bob, Ashley, and Kory.

I nervously talked most of the drive there. It was only during the last half hour that the car got uncomfortably quiet, and my heart began beating harder as we pulled into the designated hotel. Oh my goodness. Am I ready for this?

Knocking at the door

When I walked up to the front desk, I looked around to see if anyone else was in the lobby—thinking that maybe Lisa and Kevin would be checking in at the same time. The concierge asked if we were staying at the hotel for business or for fun. Not knowing how to answer his question, Bob quickly said, "Family reunion."

With that, we were given our keys and directions on how to get to our room. Once inside and somewhat settled, I tried to freshen myself up.

Why didn't I get my hair cut? My hair isn't working for me. I probably should have worn different clothes. Oh how I wish I could have lost some weight before we met.

All these self-destructive thoughts played through my head. It was as if my husband could hear my thoughts; he gave me a hug and told me I was beautiful. Giving me a kiss, he opened the door for me to walk out.

As I made my way down the hall to her room, I could feel my heart beat in my throat. I truthfully thought of running out to my car, driving off, and leaving everyone behind. I must have stood there for several minutes outside Lisa and Kevin's room door. My arm felt paralyzed. I couldn't lift it to knock on the door. I realized that if I didn't do something soon, someone was going to think I was up to no good. I quickly knocked.

And then the door opened.

There she was, in person. Lisa. Oh my goodness, she was beautiful! It was very hard to control my tears. The makeup that I had taken so long to do was now running down my face. I am sure I was such a sight.

I just stood there in front of Lisa, making note of each of her features. I took in her beautiful, brown eyes; her long, dark hair; and her small body frame—everything about her. I didn't want her to feel uncomfortable, but I couldn't stop staring. She was doing the same thing with me though. When we did lock eyes, I felt like, in some way, like I had found myself. Even her fiancé Kevin was amazed and frozen in the moment.

Oh my gosh, I was so uncomfortable. Yet I was excited. *What do I say?*

Really, what are you supposed to say in a moment like this?!

Again, my thoughts were whirling inside my head. *This is her. This is really her! Oh my gosh! What am I doing? What does she think of me?*

To tell you the truth, I am not sure what I said or if I even made sense. I think I told her a little about the situation back then and that I had wanted her to have all the things that I couldn't give her.

Lisa told me a little more about her search for me and how whenever she saw a woman with dark hair and olive complexion, she secretly asked herself, *Is that my mom?*

She had photos of herself so she could show me a timeline of her life. Still in a daze, I looked at the photos. I saw so much of myself in her. I cannot even explain the emotions I felt. Looking at the photos, I felt a mixture of regret that I had not been a part of her life and gratitude that she'd had things I could not have provided for her. I was especially grateful after Lisa shared with me that she'd had an incredible opportunity to chase her dreams and the education that she wanted. That alone gave me a sense of relief that I had made the right decision.

After about an hour (that seemed like a lifetime) I left to walk back to my room. The entire time I felt like I was holding my breath. Bob opened the door right away as he heard me fumble with the door handle. He stood staring at me, waiting for me to say something, but all I could do was exhale and cry as he gave me a hug.

I think it was the first time since that first phone call back in November that I could fully breathe.

Again, I had to fix my makeup, and we waited for Lisa and Kevin to knock on our door. I then introduced Bob and Kory. We made small talk in the room and then proceeded to the restaurant, where Ashley was waiting for us.

I understood that Ashley needed a little more time to deal with this. I couldn't make the kids love each other or even like each other. Yet that was my deepest prayer—that we could blend together and make up for lost time.

Yes, there were some very uncomfortable moments during dinner. Small talk can only last for so long. I believe we all had questions going on in each of our heads, which, from time to time, resulted in silence. So we decided to end our dinner at the Italian restaurant. We took a few pictures, gave each other hugs, and went back to our separate rooms.

CHAPTER 13

Making Up for Lost Time

The next day

We decided to meet for lunch the next day. After lunch, we roamed around the local mall, getting to know each other a little more.

This really was prefect, as it took the stress off all of us. We were *walking* with each other rather than *sitting* at the same table.

Ashley couldn't stay, but that gave Lisa, Kevin, and Kory time together. Kory, being a senior in high school at the time, wanted to check out the stores and do a little shopping. This seemed to be right up Lisa's alley, as she worked in fashion.

Bob and I stood back and watched Kory and Lisa interact with each other, and I just couldn't stop going from tears to laughter and back to tears again. The whole time, I was thinking, *Wow, Lord, you are not only restoring those areas of my past that left holes in my existence, you are, at the same time, building a new relationship I thought I could never have.*

All those years of denial and running from myself had only kept a heavy burden on me that I did not have to carry. I felt lighter, like something had been lifted off me. It is hard to explain.

All I can say is that God is so good.

♥ ♥ ♥

It was weeks after meeting Lisa, and after a host of more emails and phone calls, that I became aware of something. I was lying on my bed thinking of all that had transpired over the weeks since Lisa had been introduced into my life. I couldn't believe the relationship we were creating and that we were so connected.

Again, the inner voice spoke to my spirit: *This relationship isn't something* new. *Whether you realized it or not, you and Lisa had a relationship before—when she was growing inside of you. Remember I told you that I was restoring you. This isn't just one area of your life; it is your whole life.*

Lisa's wedding

It was all moving too fast. It wasn't even a full year since I had received that first phone call from Lisa, and now I was getting ready to go to her wedding with her closest friends and family. I couldn't even talk. I was so overwhelmed with everything!

I was instructed to go to the hotel room where Lisa and the bridal party were getting ready. As I tried to gain my composure, I found myself praying, *Lord, help me*, over and over in my head.

Again, I found myself in front of another door scared to knock; my arm felt as if it weighed a hundred pounds.

Who is inside this room I am about to enter? Lisa's closest family members and friends! Oh my word! Can I do this? I asked myself.

I can't even explain what I felt as I walked through the door. I knew everyone was waiting to see what I looked like, or at least I thought they were. When I looked around, I found a room filled with beautiful women, all of whom Lisa called family.

I said a few words to my beautiful daughter as the hairdresser worked on her beautiful, dark hair. I tried to step out the photographer's way as he clicked frantically, as if he knew the impact of the moment for me. I told her that she looked beautiful and that I was blessed beyond words that she wanted me there to be a part of her wedding day. I stayed long enough to meet everyone, and then I tried to make a graceful exit.

I returned to my own hotel room and the security of Bob's arms. I tried to rest a little before getting ready for the big moment—Lisa's wedding!

As I waited in the lineup to be escorted down the aisle, my nerves got the best of me, and my ears started to ring. I still could not believe it as I walked into a room with only three familiar faces. I tried to walk gracefully as I was announced—as Lisa's mom.

Imagine this: I had met this young woman for the first time only weeks ago. Moreover, I had just uncovered that I had been in denial about being pregnant with the baby who had blossomed into the beautiful woman that was about to get married.

As the ceremony unfolded, I had to keep pinching myself because, in my wildest dreams, I would never have believed I would be there to witness my first child's wedding.

And the wedding was stunning. Kevin and Lisa looked beautiful together. I knew they truly loved each other, especially after having seen them interact with each other when we all first met only months before. I could tell that Kevin was her strength and incredibly supportive of her. Yes, he was the answer to my (her mother's) prayer—that she had a good man in her life.

At the reception, the photographer was taking pictures of everyone as the guests settled at different tables. I wasn't sure where to sit. Ashley and Kory had brought dates, so they found random spots at different tables, but I was standing by myself.

Even Bob wasn't next to me. In the shuffle of things, we got separated, and I started to feel myself fall apart. I was so nervous. I didn't want to embarrass Lisa, or myself for that matter. Should I sit with Lisa's friends and family? Or should I sit with Kevin's? *Maybe if I slip out of the room, no one would notice*, I thought to myself.

I can only assume my feelings were written across my face because Lisa's aunt came up and gently invited me and Bob to join her at her table. *Bob is with me now. I will be okay*, I told myself. Everyone at the table was talking about the newlyweds—how beautiful the ceremony was and how gorgeous Lisa looked. Then the stories of the earlier awkward years of Lisa's life began.

As the family laughed, remembering "when," it became hard for me to keep my composure and not burst into tears at the table. I firmly nudged Bob to let me out, and I quickly made my way out into the hall. With it being a wedding reception, I didn't want anyone to see me ugly cry. But once I found a quiet, secure place alone, this is what I did.

It took me a little while to regain my pretty face so that I could walk back to the reception. By then, the music was playing, and couples were on the dance floor. I was somewhat embarrassed that I was so emotional and tried to slip back into the crowd without a scene.

However, Lisa's father-in-law must have seen that I was upset when I left the room. He walked up to me and said, "We love Lisa. She is a wonderful, sweet young lady, and we accept her as one of our own. I just want you to know that you are part of the family now too."

I smiled and thanked him for the kind words.

Then he added, "It is amazing how similar you and Lisa's mannerisms are. Your facial expressions are exactly like hers—even down to the detail that when she is about to cry she curls her bottom lip just like you do."

I am not sure why those words comforted me, but they did. I think I realized that most everyone there knew how sensitive it was for me to take this all in and that they had all extended grace to me, allowing me to be emotional.

Because of unfortunate circumstances, Lisa's adoptive parents were not there to share the day. So when it came to the part of the reception where the bride and groom dance with their father and mother, it was only Kevin and his mother on the dance floor. Then something beautiful happened. Ashley took Bob by the hand and walked him to Lisa and told them to dance.

I am not sure it was fully something that Ashley was prepared to do—to fully accept Lisa as her sister and share her daddy with her. But the gesture had a huge impact on Lisa and even Bob. I truly believe, to this day, that Ashley loves her sister Lisa and did this so that she would feel accepted.

Fighting off tears yet again, I kept my composure and enjoyed watching my *three* children dance at the reception. The photographer even took a picture of the siblings together. He said, "Okay, you three. Do something silly." Once we saw the captured moment, I couldn't believe it. In the picture, each of them reflected the same goofy expression—crossed eyes and tongues sticking out the same side of the mouth. Wow!

With all the firsts that I'd missed in Lisa's life, I felt honored that she had asked me to witness the testimony of her love for Kevin and that she wanted me to be a part of the memory that would be etched in her heart forever. What an awesome God we have. That He had given me the opportunity to be there at Lisa's wedding day was truly amazing!

Being purposeful about our family gatherings

There have been holidays, February Family Fun (FFF) weekends honoring the first time we all met in 2008, and even weddings. I cherish the times we meet, either as a family or just Lisa and me as mother and daughter. On each occasion, we make more memories that will forever fill my heart. To think about how our family has been brought together, it all seems magical, to say the least. I now believe that God had this reunion planned since that day I lay in that hospital bed heartbroken because I could not hold my baby girl. He has had His eyes on her and on me our whole lives. Even though Lisa questioned for years if she would ever meet me, God knew she would. And during all those years when I didn't realize I was walking around incomplete, God saw the day that our lives would intersect. Realizing she was the missing link to my existence, God had it all planned out—to bring healing to us both.

Even today (close to our ten-year anniversary) I type this recollection out, amazed at how my children interact together, cutting it up and being kids. At times, it seems that there weren't years between us meeting, that three of them had grown up with each other. They finish each other's sentences, have the same sense of humor, and even share the same crazy random dance moves.

Kevin, to this day, tells me that it is crazy how much he sees me in Lisa or Lisa in me. He said, "I used to think it was nurture over nature, but I can't say that now." Even now, this many years later, I sometimes get a glimpse of him watching us as he shakes his head. Amazing!

All I can say is thank you, Lord, for uniting us together. You truly do have plans to prosper us and not to harm us, to give us a future (Jeremiah 29:11).

Words from Lisa

Lisa wanted to add some words of her own, which I have not changed. After all, this telling is about her story too, though we are nowhere near saying "the end." We have so much more to explore and experience together as a family.

Here are Lisa's words:

> I don't exactly remember *when* I knew I was adopted. I honestly believe it's something I felt in my soul from the very beginning. Speaking for myself, as an adopted child, I felt this void or missing part of me, and it became magnified as I got older. I always felt lost, unwanted, and truly broken. I remember thinking that it was something I deserved because I wasn't "good enough" for my biological mom to keep. As life evolved for myself, I would push these feelings and thoughts aside. I would rarely open up about them, as I just assumed it would be something I carry with me my entire life. I would always cringe if I had to go to the doctor, who would ask for medical history. I always had to shamefully say (at the time I was ashamed) that I was adopted and had no idea about my biological family's medical history. Even though adoption has become more common, it still was something that I felt was rare and something I had to wear as a branding— "Oh, she was adopted. No one wanted her." It's really interesting to me because, even though my adoption led to self-loathing, I never blamed my bio-mom for giving me up. I would rationalize it in my head that it just didn't work out and that

was okay, but I definitely carried the blame with me for a very long time.

There were times when I would think and ask myself about my biological mom. That always amounted to wondering what she looked like, what she did, if she had a family. I also always wondered if I had siblings out there who had also been adopted. I never really wondered if she thought about me or missed me—which, looking back, was selfish.

It wasn't until after college that I really started getting curious about where I came from. I believe that came at the perfect time in my life, as I gained more stability after college—had a good job and had a positive influence in my life with my boyfriend (now husband). It was like I now had the room in my heart, soul, and mind to process what being adopted really meant. The idea of finding or reaching out to my mom came and went as I grew up. I had it in my head and convinced myself, "Why should I find her? She should find me. She was the one who gave me up after all." That was the fear of rejection coming into play, which is something I have suffered with (and still do). The fear of being told, "No, I didn't want you and still don't," really plagued me.

I eventually set my ego aside. What triggered that was that I was engaged to get married. This was supposed to be one of the happiest times in a woman's life, but I was an emotional mess. I felt broken and lost. I would read books or watch shows where the bride-to-be goes dress shopping with her mom or her mom throws her an engagement party or bridal shower, and I felt sorry for myself because I did not have that. I also felt ashamed because my fiancé had this broken woman who had no family. And I felt that I didn't come from anything good. I wasn't bringing anything to the table, so to speak. It was just me. (Now I realize that it was enough. But at the time, I did not feel worthy to be marrying an amazing man).

I remember one evening, I was sitting and watching TV, and my now husband turned it off and told me that I needed to find my biological mom or at least try. He told me that I came from something good and there was unconditional love out there (aside from his) and that my mom thought about me and missed me. He said I had to set aside my fear and anger and try. He assured me that he was there for me no matter what—he knew the fear of rejection was paralyzing me. I thought, *Fine. What do I have to lose?*

Nothing was the answer. I had very minimal information regarding my adoption. I knew I was from a small community in Michigan, that my mom was young, and that I was Filipino. It was a very random assortment of facts! Of course, in the day and age of social media and Googling, we tried to Google search old yearbooks from schools in that area and so on.

After a few attempts, we decided to make this search legitimate. I went through the process (which is fairly easy) and filled out the paperwork and so forth. The process part is in a haze. I just remember doing it, talking to people, and then waiting. I was told that my file would either be open or closed, and it was up to the birth mom. Open meant that she had allowed information to be shared. Closed meant it was a dead end, and I would have to pursue other avenues for contact (a private investigator).

I don't remember how long it took to hear back from the central adoption registry, but I was preoccupied with wedding planning—thankfully, I was distracted. Then one day, I got the mail, and I had a thick envelope from the probate court and registry. I immediately started shaking. This was it! The moment of truth. What had my mom decided for our fate?!

Kevin and I opened it up together and discovered the file was *open*! I was excited, but then came fear: *Oh no. Wow. This is now very real. What am I to do with this information? What if this is a mean joke? What if she sees me or hears from me and decides she regrets having made this decision?* I had so many thoughts and emotions that I remember wanting to just lie down. We read through all the information, including a short bio about me and my mom and the circumstances. It's like the walls were closing in on me.

It was at that moment that I realized my mom didn't really have a choice. She was very young and had placed me for adoption in the hopes for me to have a better life. Immediately, my heart filled with admiration and pride. It was a selfless act. That very evening, I called the phone number provided. I was operating on pure adrenalin. I didn't have what I wanted to say thought out. I had no idea the possibility of her being married or having other children. I just called! I did it—I got the courage to just call.

There is no way to accurately describe the emotions I felt as I called my mom for the very first time—at twenty-six years old. I am often asked to describe what it was like, and all I can say is it was surreal, and then there are no other words. The conversation was very short, shocking, and emotional. Looking back, I didn't realize the magnitude of this first step. I had no expectations going into it. The only thing I really wanted to know was what did my mom look like, did I look like her, and what medical history I should know about—very basic things.

At the time, I had no expectations of emotional healing. I didn't even want to put that out there as an expectation because I did not want to be disappointed. My attitude was, let's just see what she looks like and if there are any issues, and then that is it. Eventually we exchanged pictures. *Wow*, this was the moment I had been waiting for—what did she look like. I sat staring at her picture and thought she was beautiful, and we looked very similar. I felt a sense of pride—she looked healthy and happy! I learned in our phone conversation that I had a half brother and a half sister. I never even anticipated that! It wasn't a thought of mine that I might have actual siblings! I received their pictures as well and stared at those forever. We looked alike! We all looked alike—there was no denying that I was her daughter, and these were my siblings. I instantly got so excited. I wanted to know more. I wanted to meet them and her. My fear of rejection left. I was so excited that I had *found* my family. I had found my sense of belonging for my core foundation, and there are no words in the world that can describe that. My void has been filled.

The days leading up to the actual meeting were stressful. I was a mess. I had the fears of rejection creeping back: What if she thinks I am weird, dumb, ugly, fat, and on and on—really superficial things? What if my siblings hated me? I tried so hard to see things from their point of view. All of a sudden, they have a sister! *Whoa*. That is some heavy stuff! I wanted more than anything for them to realize that I was not replacing them. I just wanted to know where I came from.

The time had come for us to meet face-to-face. There is no way to prepare for such an event. I remember opening the hotel room door and just staring in shock and then crying. There she was—my mom! This was a moment I had been thinking about my entire life, but I never really thought it would happen. If we had just sat and stared at each other, I would have been fine with that. It was just me taking the time to actually absorb what was happening.

I eventually met my brother and sister. Same exact reaction. Something I did not anticipate was the comfort and ease I had with everyone. It was like I was this little missing puzzle piece. It felt right—it felt like I was at home.

This now has happened almost ten years ago. My relationships with my mom, brother, and sister have evolved. It's surreal that when we are all together it's like we have never been apart. We laugh and cry and operate as if we have been a family together this entire time. I am so grateful and proud to talk about my mom, my sister, and my brother! My love for all of them is so gigantic. I often have to pinch myself when we are together and remind myself, *Hey, this is your family. They love and have accepted you.*

Regardless, I still struggle with the concept of having a mom. I never had a mom. I didn't have a person to go to when I needed advice or help with problems or just to talk to. I never had that figure in my life, and as an adult, it's difficult for me to acknowledge that I now have this. It's something I realize I need to work on and continue to process. I may never get to that quintessential definition of a mother-daughter relationship—and that is okay for me. This whole story and situation is everything but normal. I have to continue to have no expectations and enjoy the ride—enjoy being loved and loving a mom, brother, and sister unconditionally.

Like anything in life, this continues to be a journey for me. The journey of processing and healing will never end, but it has been a journey nothing short of magical. I am beyond grateful for having had the courage and support to take the chance–the result has only been beautiful.

CHAPTER 14

_____

Message to Birth Moms

Placing your child up for adoption is not an easy thing. In your head, you know it is for the best for your baby, but your heart is torn. You may experience great depression because you never got to hold your baby. Grief may overwhelm you as you remember your child's birth and how you were not able to comfort his or her cries. You may experience heartache, as I did, especially on birthdays, but never be able to acknowledge this pain openly. When your child's birth date approaches, you may become melancholy. Like I did, you may push those feelings down deep, denying that the decision you made back then has an effect on you now.

Perhaps you briefly searched the internet for some sort of support group, without success. Words and phrases—*abandon*, *neglect*, *you're a bad mom*, or, worse, *you don't deserve to be a mother*—haunt you, and you become supersensitive about your parenting skills.

You may experience extreme guilt or shame and believe that the child (no matter what age) is better off not knowing about you. Or you may convince yourself your child will never forgive you or ever want to meet you.

You may paint pictures in your head of how wonderful your

child is doing in his or her life without you. And you see yourself as being outside looking in at your life and feel as if you aren't even a part of your own existence.

Keeping the secret of your child's existence and your grief over the loss of that child as part of your daily life becomes harder as you are raising his or her siblings. You often find yourself wondering when would be a good time, if ever, to share your heartache with your family.

You do not have to carry this alone. And you do not need to be afraid of allowing these emotions out. I understand it is hard to permit something to surface that you may have purposely stuffed for years. But, truly, God heals the brokenhearted and binds up their wounds if we allow Him to (Psalm 147:3).

You might have felt a tug on your heart as you read my testimony but remained afraid to look over your shoulder. I understand. It took me twenty-six years before I even realized I was running from something—myself. But know this: God is gentle, and He never forces us to do something. He is truly with you every step of the way of uncovering those things of your past.

Over time, I had received healing of some of the scars and divots on my heart, but it was time to fill in that hole that had long been buried deep in my heart's center. God was so gracious to bring a few women alongside me to help me through the process.

If you feel you're at a place in your life where you can allow Him to have all those areas of hurts, He will take care of you. God will restore what has been lost—self-worth, peace, joy, and unconditional love.

As I searched for resources to help you on this journey of healing, I was somewhat disappointed that I wasn't finding much. I did, however, find a book by Lindsay Arielle, *How a Birth Mom Healed: A Diary*. Her story is different from mine (her child's adoption was open), but we have a common heart—healing for birth moms.

As an answer to both our prayers, the Lord led our paths to each other. Our desire is to one day create resources to help you (the birth parent) along your own journey. However, until then, if you would like to reach out to me, please do. You can email me at georgia@2liftuup.com.

If you're interested in reading more about my expedition of faith and to find future books (once completed), check out www.2liftuup.com.

CONCLUSION

With all that I have been through, I still believe wholeheartedly that placing my baby girl for adoption was the best option for me.

Yes, I made the decision at a young age and had no idea how it would impact my life overall.

Yes, I felt judged. Yes, I was regarded as being selfish and even irresponsible among my peers. But those are all lies!

My belief is that each life that is being developed inside a womb is not just there by chance and that God knows each person.

As we read in Psalm 139:15–16, "You watched me as I was being formed in utter seclusion, as I was woven together in the dark of the womb. You saw me before I was born. Every day of my life was recorded in your book. Every moment was laid out before a single day had passed" (New Living Translation).

I also believe wholeheartedly that God has appointed specific people to help each of us through a journey of healing. So if you find that any part of my story resonates inside you and you have no one to reach out to, I want to encourage you to reach out to me. Just email and make the subject line "Reaching Out."

My prayer for those who find themselves at a crossroads, trying to decide

Dear heavenly Father, You know each person involved in this decision. You know the plans and purpose of each life, and You also know the emotions involved. Lord God, open the heavens over these lives and give them Your perspective. I pray for armies of angels to encamp around them and equip them with everything they need to fulfill the purposes You have for them. Shower them with unconditional love. Lastly, Lord, bring those specific people You have handpicked to come alongside them as they walk out this journey. We ask these things in Jesus's name. Amen.

Printed in the United States
By Bookmasters